S0-CAV-760

IT'S NOT JUST SPINACH

The vegetarian way of eating is incredibly varied, employing such exotic, appealing foods as

> calcium-rich *hijiki*—an unforgettably delicious appetizer
> *tempeh* from Indonesia—vitamin-rich, and with more protein than steak
> *tofu*—totally versatile as a food on its own or an added enhancement to others

With these—along with fresh vegetables, herbs and natural seasonings—you can prepare delicious dishes as hearty as any meat stew or roast.

For economy, health and true gourmet enjoyment, try vegetarian eating—and the wealth of information and guidance in

TOTAL VEGETARIAN COOKING

Keats Books of Relevant Interest

Add a Few Sprouts by Martha Oliver

Bonnie Fisher's Way With Herbs Cookbook

Children's Diet Book by M. Bircher-Benner, M.D.

The Getting Back to Nature Diet by Salem Kirban

Good Food Naturally by John B. Harrison

The Herb Tea Book by Dorothy Hall

Hunza Health Secrets by Renée Taylor

Mental and Elemental Nutrients by Carl C. Pfeiffer, Ph.D., M.D.

Minerals and Your Health by Len Mervyn, Ph.D.

Minnie Muenscher's Herb Cookbook

Nutrients to Age Without Senility by Abram Hoffer, M.D., Ph.D. and Morton Walker, D.P.M.

Orthomolecular Nutrition by Abram Hoffer, M.D., Ph.D. and Morton Walker, D.P.M.

The Prevention of Incurable Disease by M. Bircher-Benner, M.D.

The Raw Fruits and Vegetables Book by Max E. Bircher, M.D. and M. Bircher-Benner, M.D.

Soybeans for Health and a Longer Life by Philip S. Chen, Ph.D.

Super Soy! by Barbara Farr

What Herbs Are All About by Jack Joseph Challem and Renate Lewin-Challem

What's In It For You: Carlson Wade's Shopper's Guide to Health Stores

Whole-Grain Baking Sampler by Beatrice Trum Hunter

Yogurt, Kefir and Other Milk Cultures by Beatrice Trum Hunter

NATHANIEL ALTMAN'S

TOTAL VEGETARIAN COOKING

Keats Publishing, Inc. New Canaan, Connecticut

Neither the author nor the publisher has authorized the use of their names or the use of any material contained in this book in connection with the sale, promotion or advertising of any product or apparatus. Any such use is strictly unauthorized and in violation of the rights of Nathaniel Altman and Keats Publishing, Inc.

NATHANIEL ALTMAN'S TOTAL VEGETARIAN COOKING

Pivot Original Edition published 1981

Copyright © 1981 by Nathaniel Altman

All Rights Reserved
No part of this book may be copied or reproduced without the written consent of the publisher.

Library of Congress Catalog Number: 80-85343
Printed in the United States of America

PIVOT ORIGINAL HEALTH BOOKS are published by
Keats Publishing, Inc., 36 Grove Street (Box 876)
New Canaan, Connecticut 06840

Contents

Acknowledgments

The author gratefully acknowledges permission to use material from the following corporations:

Fearn Soya Foods, Melrose Park, Illinois, for material obtained from their Composition of Foods Chart.

Table 4.19 is reprinted from *Complete Book of Vitamins* © 1966 by Rodale Press, Inc. Permission granted by Rodale Press, Inc., Emmaus, PA 18049.

The Macmillan Co. for quotations from C.M. Taylor and O.F. Pye's *Foundations of Nutrition*, sixth edition.

The Nilgiri Press; food values for folacin and vitamin B-12 reprinted by permission from *Laurel's Kitchen: A Handbook for Vegetarian Cookery and Nutrition* by Laurel Robertson, Carol Flinders and Bronwen Godfrey, © 1976 by Nilgiri Press, Petaluma CA 94953.

I would also like to express my gratitude to my aunt, Mildred Aissen, for her valued assistance in creating, testing and criticizing the recipes (based on her forty-five years as an excellent cook); and to Leonita Lovett, Edward Gasser, Linda James, Dixy Mahy, Freya Dinshah, José Alberto Rosa, Lou Ann Yonish and my mother, Sadie Altman, for their recipe ideas and suggestions.

PREFACE

EATING FOR HEALTH CAN BE
EATING FOR PLEASURE

NEXT TO SEX, we probably think more about food than
anything else. We dream about it, talk about it, and
read about it in magazines, cookbooks and diet guides.
When we aren't actually eating, we are looking forward
to our next meal or snack. While our primary reason for
eating is to survive, there is no doubt that eating is one
of our greatest sources of pleasure.

Unfortunately, for many, food is a major source of
pain. Our predilection for lots of stimulating and heavy
foods like red meat, saturated fat, white flour products,
refined sugar and other highly processed items has
promoted a wide variety of diet-related diseases that
have reached epidemic proportions in this country. They
range from relatively minor problems like acid indigestion and occasional constipation to life-threatening diseases like hypertension, obesity, cancer and diabetes.
Although there is no reason to deny the legitimate
pleasure we can derive from an attractive and delicious .
meal, how much pleasure do we really have when we
eat foods we know are not good for us?

Today millions of Americans (as well as Canadians,
Europeans, Australians and New Zealanders) are be-

ginning to question our typical way of eating. They recognize the need for a more natural diet based on plant-oriented foods that are simple to prepare, enjoyable to eat, and which provide good nutrition at reasonable cost. Since vegetarian foods are rich in essential nutrients and dietary fiber, they are especially appealing for those who want good food value for their money. And since these foods are relatively free from pesticide residues and cholesterol, it is no surprise that meat-free diets have become extremely popular in recent years.

Since I wrote my first book on vegetarianism, *Eating for Life*, nearly a decade ago, the vegetarian image in America has changed considerably. From rather humble and dull beginnings, vegetarian cuisine has evolved into a highly sophisticated and exciting art. Dozens of good cookbooks have been written to help make any cook a vegetarian gourmet chef, while vegetarian recipes and menu ideas are regularly published in magazines like *Woman's Day*, *Family Circle* and *Redbook*. Vegetarian dinner lines have sprung up at colleges and universities around the country, while almost every city in America features at least one restaurant where diners can enjoy a wholesome vegetarian meal. Entertainers like Efrem Zimbalist, Jr., Cloris Leachman, Dennis Weaver, Susan St. James, Lola Falana, Nick Nolte and the Captain and Tenille have added a touch of glamour to the vegetarian image, while athletes like Bill Walton, Chip Oliver and marathon runner Amby Burfoot have shown that we can be successful in athletics without eating a steak at every meal. Nutritionists like Dr. Jean Mayer and Dr. Mark Hegsted have written that vegetarian diets can be good for our bodies while religious leaders like Swami Satchidananda, Sri Chitrabhanu and the Dalai Lama have taught that a diet without meat is good for the soul.

Many vegetarian books have appeared over the past ten years. Some, like *Eating for Life*, were basically scholarly works which stressed the ethical, cultural and philosophical aspects of vegetarianism. Others, like *Diet for a Small Planet*, focussed on the world food situation and how to balance your proteins.

During my class in vegetarianism at The New School for Social Research in New York City, I discovered that there was a need for a different kind of vegetarian book that would offer simple and practical "how to" advice towards enjoying a healthy, economical and pleasurable vegetarian way of living. The book would need to explore what a vegetarian diet is and what it is not; how a meatless diet can keep us healthy, how we can save money on food, and how to obtain adequate vitamins, minerals and protein without having an advanced degree in applied chemistry.

The book would also need to explore the medicinal value of common vegetarian foods and how they can keep us healthy. It would need to take us to a health food store and explore the wide variety of uncommon foods like tempeh, tofu, miso and tamari. The book would help us identify common food additives and see which are good for us and which are harmful. Finally, the book would need to offer an abundance of diet plans and healthy recipes that would show how to prepare gourmet meals at rock-bottom prices.

Total Vegetarian Cooking has been designed to satisfy these needs. Enjoy it in good health!

NATHANIEL ALTMAN
Brooklyn, New York
July 1981

SECTION I

Vegetarianism:
Foundations

Chapter 1

VEGETARIAN ROOTS

ACCORDING to a recent Roper poll, more than 7 million Americans are practicing vegetarians while another 37 million are cutting down on the meat they eat. Nevertheless, a random survey of people on the street reveals a great deal of confusion about what a vegetarian actually is:

"A vegetarian eats only vegetables."

"My sister's a vegetarian. She eats everything but beef and pork. Loves chicken and fish."

"They eat only raw foods in special combinations."

"No meat, fish, eggs or dairy products."

"Vegetarians eat fish."

"Aren't they the ones who eat just beans and brown rice?"

The big three

Basically speaking, a vegetarian does not eat any part of anyone who can walk, run, crawl, swim or fly. This includes meat, fats and gelatin from cattle and calves, as well as pork, poultry, fish and crustacea (including shrimp, clams and lobster).

Vegetarians can be divided into three major groups. *Lacto-ovo-vegetarians* eat eggs and dairy products in addition to plant foods, while *lacto-vegetarians* use dairy products but abstain from eggs. Pure vegetarians or *vegans* will not eat any foods of animal origin, including meat, milk, eggs, animal fats, gelatin and honey. Many also refuse to use any leather or wool, and will not attend any events (such as the circus) where animal exploitation occurs. By far the most enthusiastic vegetarians, vegans often include a wide variety of grains, legumes, seeds, nuts, fruits and vegetables in their diets, as well as sea vegetables, sprouts and tofu.

The vast majority of vegetarians are of the lacto-ovo or lacto varieties, while perhaps one vegetarian in fifty is a strict vegan. While most vegetarians are quite disciplined, some lacto-ovo-vegetarians may eat a piece of chicken now and then, or a vegan may occasionally succumb to the temptation of an ice cream cone on a hot summer day. For reasons of clarity, many people prefer to call themselves *primarily* vegetarian or *primarily* vegan rather than force themselves to maintain a standard they are unable to live up to.

People become vegetarians for a variety of reasons. Some stop eating meat because they don't want to kill animals for food, while others simply don't like the taste of meat. Ecologically-minded individuals give up meat to help save the environment, while the diet-conscious give up meat to help save their waistline. Some people go vegetarian because they feel it is good for the soul, while others become vegetarians because they feel plant foods are good for the body. Some may become vegetarians to save money on food, while others become vegetarians to save time in the kitchen.

New blossoms, old roots

While vegetarianism has enjoyed an unprecedented period of growth in recent years, most people are unaware that meat-free diets trace their history to the earliest years of human civilization.

Our involvement with a vegetarian diet appears to extend at least as far as the time of Paranthropus, when our early ancestors ate no meat except during periods of crisis.

The Ice Age is recognized as a principal factor that forced early Homo Sapiens to eat animal flesh in order to survive. The custom of meat-eating has continued throughout history, due to necessity (as with the Eskimos) or through habit, cultural pressure or lack of knowledge. Nevertheless, vegetarianism has been regarded as the natural diet of humans since the beginning of recorded history. The *Encyclopedia of Religion and Morals* tells us that the ancient Egyptians and Greeks knew the religious form of vegetarianism, and that their myths (like those in Palestine) represented the human as having been originally a fruit-eating creature.

In ancient Greece such figures as Plato, Diogenes and the great mathematician and sage Pythagoras were strong advocates for a meatless diet, while in India the Buddha stressed the doctrine of *Ahimsa*—harmlessness to all living things. Today many of his 400 million followers are strict vegetarians, especially the priests. In early Roman times, Seneca, Virgil, Ovid and the poet Horace advocated and practiced the vegetarian way of living.

The Bible clearly states in Genesis I:29 what our natural diet was intended to be:

> And God said, "Behold, I have given you every herb bearing seed, which is upon the face of all the earth, and every tree, in which is the fruit of a tree yielding seed; to you it shall be for meat."

The advantages of a vegetarian diet were also discussed in the book of Daniel I:12-17, and in the famous Epistle of St. Paul to the Romans: "It is good neither to eat flesh . . . nor any thing whereby thy brother stumbleth, or is offended, or is made weak."

The Essene Gospel of Peace, a direct translation of early Aramaic texts, recounts the vegetarian message of Jesus Christ:

> And the flesh of slain beasts in his body will become his own tomb. For I tell you truly, he who kills, kills himself, and whoso eats the flesh of slain beasts, eats the body of death.

Other ancient religious writings reflect similar positions on the eating of meat. According to the Vedic book of wisdom, the *Laws of Manu*:

> Meat can never be obtained without injury to living creatures and injury to sentient beings is detrimental to (the attainment of) heavenly bliss; let him therefore shun (the use of) meat.

Many of the world's outstanding writers, artists, scientists, philosophers, teachers and spiritual leaders have either advocated or adopted a vegetarian diet. They include Plutarch, Porphyry, William Shakespeare, Leonardo da Vinci, Sir Isaac Newton, Jean Jacques Rousseau, François Voltaire, Benjamin Franklin, Charles Darwin, General William Booth, Henry David Thoreau, Richard Wagner, Ralph Waldo Emerson, Percy Bysshe Shelley, Alexander Pope, Horace Greeley, Rabindranath Tagore, Susan B. Anthony, Leo Tolstoy, Upton Sinclair, H.G. Wells, Albert Einstein, Annie Besant, George Bernard Shaw, General George Montgomery, Albert Schweitzer, M.K. Gandhi, J. Krishnamurti, Isaac Bashevis Singer and His Holiness the Dalai Lama.

Vegetarians are often reminded that Adolph Hitler was a vegetarian for several years while he tried to cure his chronic stomach ailments. However, according to a personal account by one of his closest associates, Albert

Speer, Hitler's vegetarianism was an illusion. In his book *Inside the Third Reich*, Speer wrote that Hitler had a weakness for meat-filled ravioli and was especially fond of the sausage to be had in Munich's butcher shops.

Many religions, as well as other spiritually-oriented groups, have advocated (officially and unofficially) a vegetarian diet for either health, ethical or religious reasons. They include the Theosophical Order of Service, the Adventist Church, the Essene, Hindu, Buddhist, Zoroastrian, Tao and Jain faiths, the Hare Krishna movement, the Unity Church, The Order of the Cross, the Liberal Catholic Church, The United Society of Believers (Shakers), the Trappist, St. Benedict and Carthusian orders of the Roman Catholic Church, as well as other Christian organizations like the Universal Christian Gnostic Movement and the Rosicrucian Fellowship.

Sowing the seeds: the vegetarian movement

Shortly after the term *vegetarian* (from the Greek term *vegetas* or "full of life") was introduced in 1842, the first organization devoted to promoting a meat-free diet was formed in England. However in 1817, Rev. William Metcalfe and forty-one vegetarian members of his Bible Christian Church sailed from England to settle in Philadelphia. The group's philosophy was strengthened through the influence of Dr. Reuben D. Mussey (fourth president of the American Medical Association) and Dr. Edward Hitchcock, president of Amherst College. The Rev. Sylvester Graham, whose research in grains led to the use of Graham (unbolted) flour for baking, and Dr. J. H. Kellogg, founder of the Battle Creek Sanitarium and pioneer of the breakfast food industry, were among the most enthusiastic supporters of the vegetarian movement in America.

The world's largest vegetarian organization is the International Vegetarian Union (I.V.U.). Formed in 1908, it is composed of over fifty affiliated national groups around the world. Every two years the I.V.U. sponsors the World Vegetarian Congress, which is designed to share vegetarian teaching with the public, as well as to help vegetarian activists make contacts with other vegetarian individuals and groups around the world. The United States hosted its first World Vegetarian Congress in 1975.

Active vegetarian societies are working throughout the world, and provide reliable information about the nutritional, economic and ethical aspects of vegetarian living. A basic listing of these organizations and vegetarian publications can be found in an appendix to this book.

The past few years have witnessed a groundswell of interest in natural living and vegetarian diets in particular. From all indications, the move towards plant-oriented fare will increase as more people discover that vegetarianism is not a passing fad, but a practical, cheap, healthy and pleasurable way of living. Let's find out why millions of people have decided to give up meat and move toward the vegetarian alternative.

Chapter 2

WHY VEGETARIANISM?

WHEN Ken M. was a child, he felt guilty about eating animals, and he wouldn't eat steak, roast beef, fish fillets or turkey legs because they reminded him of the animal the foods came from. By the time he graduated from high school, Ken had become a strict vegetarian.

Eileen E. became active in the ecology movement as a Girl Scout counselor. When she learned that a meat-oriented diet uses far more land, water and petroleum than a plant-based diet, she gave up meat and reduced her consumption of dairy products.

When Robert P. visited Latin America, he found out that much of the best cropland was used to raise cattle for export to the United States and Europe. At the same time, local people went hungry because the amount of land used to grow staple foods like beans and rice was reduced and food prices skyrocketed. To free himself from complicity in this situation, Robert became a vegetarian.

Although most people decide to become vegetarians in order to save money or to avoid heart disease and other health problems linked to meat, other factors like ecology, ethics and the world food situation follow close behind.

Saving the earth: vegetarianism and ecology

Within the past few years, increasing air, water and land pollution has brought the issue of ecology—our relationship with the environment—into sharp focus. People from every part of the world are slowly beginning to realize that unless we learn to conserve, respect, and protect the natural resources of the earth, every living inhabitant of this planet will perish from lack of pure water, clean air and fertile land.

As more and more data reveal that a meat-oriented diet wreaks havoc on the air, water and land—while using enormous amounts of non-renewable energy and water resources—a growing number of ecologists have adopted the vegetarian way of life.

Every aspect of meat production—from raising livestock animals to the slaughtering process—creates serious problems for the environment. For example, raising crops for animal feed is a primary cause of chemical pollution. Because we have become highly dependent on chemical fertilizers to improve feed crop yields, certain chemicals (like nitrogen) have seeped into the water supply and have caused severe pollution.

The problem of water pollution is compounded by the problem of animal grazing—a phenomenon which has resulted in severe land erosion throughout the world. Overgrazing was an important factor in the creation of the "Dust Bowl" in the 1930s, while intensive grazing was a major contributor to the recent destruction of land in the African nations of Chad, Mali, Mauritania, Niger, Senegal and Upper Volta during the last decade.

A still graver problem stems from the feedlots where animals are fattened up with concentrated feeds before slaughter. There are over 200,000 feedlots in the United States, Canada and Mexico, and these range in size from a small corral holding a dozen animals to a mammoth operation in which several thousand animals are fed at one time. According to Dr. Harold Bernard, an agricultural expert with the United States Environmental Protection Agency, "(Feedlot) runoffs carry wastes that are ten to several hundred times more concentrated than raw domestic sewage."

When the highly concentrated wastes in a runoff flow into a stream or river, the results can be—and frequently are—catastrophic. The amount of dissolved oxygen in the waterway will be sharply reduced, while levels of ammonia, nitrates, phosphates and bacteria soar.

After the animal is fattened up at the feedlot, it is taken to the slaughterhouse to be killed. If you venture to any of the eight thousand slaughterhouses in North America, you'll understand why the meat industry is considered one of the most arrogant pollutors of the air, landscape and waterways.

Environmental pollution and the meat industry was discussed by Dr. A. Jepsen of the Institute of Hygiene and Microbiology in Denmark at a Food and Agriculture Organization of the United Nations (FAO) Seminar on the Development of Meat Production, Hygiene, Technology and Marketing:

> Drainage from slaughterhouses and meatworks carry water having a high load of organic materials . . . It also contains pathogens, number and species depend on the epidemiological status of the animal population of that particular area. Tubercle bacilli, Salmonella and helminth eggs, especially Ascaris suum eggs are common findings. Conventional and newer sewage purification processes . . . do not solve the problem of preventing pathogens from entering the aquatic recipients.

To compound the problem of water pollution, ecologists point out that meat eaters consume more than their fair share of the pure water that is still available for our use. When we consider the per capita consumption of our scarce water resources, we must bear in mind certain factors: the water used to irrigate feed crops, the drinking water for livestock, the water used in slaughterhouse operation, and the water used to wash and prepare our food before we eat it. In his book *Proteins: Their Chemistry and Politics* Dr. Aaron Altschul points out that the all-vegetable (or vegan) diet requires 300 gallons of water per person per day, while the mixed animal and vegetable diet requires 2500 gallons. He adds that the cost of water per pound of meat is about twenty-five times that of the cost for a pound of vegetables.

Animal agriculture and energy

Most of us overlook the fact that our eating habits can affect the world and domestic energy situation. An article in the February 1976 issue of *American Scientist* forecasted that if our present rate of meat consumption continues, we will need an additional 29 million barrels of oil by the year 2000.

When we consider the actual calories of energy needed to produce one calorie of food, the vegetarian diet is very economical. In order to produce one calorie of feedlot beef, 10 calories of energy are required. The corresponding figures for "factory-farmed" eggs is 3; milk, 1; soybeans, .50, intensively-grown corn, .45; and intensively-grown rice, only .15.

Vegetarianism: ending the world food shortage

One of the main causes of the world food shortage is the inability of an animal diet to give people an adequate return for land used. According to Dr. K.E. Hunt, Director of the Agricultural Economics Institute and the Institute of Agrarian Affairs in Oxford, England:

Even the most efficient livestock provide in their products no more than a small fraction of the nutrients they consume. Consequently a community which is definitely short of food, cannot, without aggravating the shortage, feed to livestock any plant products which the people could eat themselves. Nor can they use, for their livestock, any land which could, by feasible adjustment of farming practice, be made to provide food for humans.

The following conversion table illustrates the inefficiency of how animals convert plant foods into protein:

Table 2.1

CONVERSION OF ANNUAL FOOD PROTEIN TO ANNUAL PRODUCT PROTEIN AT HIGH PRODUCTIVITY LEVELS FOR DIFFERENT LIVESTOCK CLASSES

Class	Production Level	Annual Crude Protein Yield (Pounds)	Annual Crude Protein Consumed (Pounds)	Efficiency %
Cow	1500 gallons at 3.25% protein	490	1290	38
Hen	320 eggs at 13% protein	5	16	31
Broiler	6 crops at 4 lb. 1 wt.	2.5	8	31
Fish	One acre carp, warm pond	1500	7500	20
Rabbit	4 litters of 10 at 3 pound carcass	18	105	17
Pork	2¼ litters of 12 at 90 lb. carcass	270	1850	15
Lamb	2 litters of 3 at 35 pound carcass	24	275	9
Steer	650 pound carcass	75	1250	6

Source: P. N. Wilson, *Biological Ceilings and Economic Efficiencies for the Production of Animal Protein*, Chemistry and Industry, No. 27, July 6, 1968.

Economists tell us that by eliminating our dependency on a meat-oriented diet, we are able to make much better use of productive land. An acre of land producing feed for cattle, hogs, poultry or milk can provide a moderately active adult with protein requirements for less than 250 days. An acre devoted to dry edible beans will take care of his or her protein needs for over 1100 days, while soybeans will satisfy protein needs for over 2200 days—a ratio of ten to one over beef.

Dr. Lyle P. Sherz wrote in *Foreign Affairs*: "The billion people in the rich nations, with Cadillac tastes for livestock products, use practically as much cereal as feed to livestock as the two billion people in the low income nations use directly as food."

There has been mounting controversy over the exportation of corn, wheat, soybeans and other basic foods to the developing or Third World countries. This trend of feeding animals imported grains is now beginning to catch on in the Third World countries. During a recent year, Bolivia fed 410,000 metric tons of grain to animals, while Haiti—one of the poorest countries of the world with an extremely high rate of starvation—fed 300,000 tons of grain to animals. During the same year, Haiti exported over 600 tons of meat to the United States. In Guatemala for example, where 75 percent of the children under five are malnourished, nearly thirty million pounds of meat were exported to the United States during 1980.

While the possibility of a huge world food deficit is a source of depression for many people, the direct consumption of plant foods can solve the problem completely. Coupled with fair and efficient distribution, the production of soybeans, wheat, rice, corn, beans and potatoes is more than adequate to feed a hungry world.

There are many ethical reasons why vegetarians won't eat meat, but a major argument involves the way animals are raised for food. In order to produce the most meat at the highest profit, animals are force-fed chemical feed mixtures and injected with a variety of hormones and animal drugs. This not only destroys their natural habits and instincts, but alters their metabolism and changes their body chemistry. Crossbreeding has, over many years, produced animals which bear a sorry resemblance to the agile, independent creatures they might have been if left in their natural state, if permitted to flourish in small numbers.

As farms have become animal factories, many creatures—especially pigs, chickens and calves—never see the light of day until they are taken to the slaughterhouse. When I visited a modern pig farm, I saw over one hundred sows kept immobilized and confined to tiny stalls in a closed, overcrowded room. I was told that their main activities involved eating, gaining weight, getting pregnant through artificial insemination, and nursing their young. Bearing in mind that the pig is considered to be as intelligent as the family dog, such confinement is sheer torture.

Calves are routinely taken from their mothers before they are a day old and live for six to eight weeks until they are butchered for veal. Dairy cows are kept as long as they are good milk producers, after which they are slaughtered for meat.

Chickens are perhaps the most cruelly treated of all animals. Often kept in windowless climate-controlled sheds, they spend their eight-to-nine-week life in extremely cramped and stress-producing conditions, with often four birds squeezed into one 18″ × 24″ cage. According to the book *Animal Liberation*:

> Feather-pecking and cannibalism have increased to a formidable extent of late years, due, no doubt, to . . . boredom, overcrowding in badly ventilated houses . . . lack of feeding space, unbalanced food or shortage of water, and heavy infestation of insect pests.

There are several excellent books which discuss the subject of intensive animal raising in great detail. Consult the recommended reading section of this book for guidance.

On death and dying

Ethical vegetarians believe that if every meat eater witnessed the slaughtering process, nearly everyone would convert to vegetarianism overnight. While their belief may be exaggerated, the fact remains that observing the death of an animal in a slaughterhouse is an experience one can never forget.

Briefly stated, hogs are forced onto a conveyor belt with an electric prod (which is capable of producing first degree burns). The conveyor takes the animal through a chamber of carbon dioxide gas which renders it unconscious. As it leaves the chamber, it is brought on the belt to the "sticker" whose job is to cut the animal's throat. For other large animals, most slaughterhouses use a device which gives the animal a high voltage electric shock, or use mechanical stunners which penetrate the skull and brain. Another type of captive bolt stunner employs on the captive bolt a device known as a "mushroom head." The mushroom-headed bolt delivers a knockout blow to the head without penetrating the skull. Then the animal is brought to the "sticker" to be killed.

All animals destined for Kosher slaughter are killed without stunning, and are killed by a trained rabbi who tries to sever both the windpipe and jugular vein in one quick incision.

While most animals are stunned before slaughter, no one can deny the fear, rage and pain involved in their death. Over 110 million cattle, calves, sheep, lambs and pigs are killed in the United States every year, in addition to over three billion chickens, turkeys and ducks.

Chapter 3

FROM CIRCULATION TO SEX:
A VEGETARIAN DIET
IS GOOD FOR YOU

MANY early vegetarians—like Leonardo Da Vinci, Tolstoy, George Bernard Shaw and the poet Shelley— felt that meat eating was immoral and that they would even risk nutritional deficiency and disease rather than eat animals for food. To their surprise, however, their health flourished and with the exception of Shelley— who died at the age of thirty-one by accidental drowning —they enjoyed extremely long, healthy and productive lives.

The fear that a diet without meat will lead to deficiencies and disease has kept many people from trying a vegetarian diet, as they flock to the meat counter for the protein, vitamins and minerals they feel only meat is able to provide. However a growing number of Americans, Canadians, Europeans and Australians have discovered that a vegetarian diet not only meets their nutritional needs but can have a positive impact on their health as well. They appreciate the fact that a vegetarian diet contains far less animal drugs, chemical additives and pesticide residues than meat, and provides more dietary fiber, less fat and less cholesterol than a meat-oriented diet.

Recent studies show that vegetarians enjoy a longer life expectancy than meat-eaters do, and that a diet without meat can lower the risk of hypertension, heart attack, stroke and several forms of cancer. A high-carbohydrate and low-fat vegetarian diet increases our endurance in sports and other physical activities, while its cleansing and sensitizing properties enhance our ability to enjoy music, art, a walk in the woods and even sex. The fact that many Hollywood personalities like Gloria Swanson, Susan St. James, Candice Bergen and Dennis Weaver have found that a vegetarian diet helps keep them trim and young looking has led others to try the vegetarian alternative to improve self-image and psychological well-being. According to Robert Rodale, the editor of *Prevention* and one of America's most respected health educators:

> Vegetarians today tend to eat a remarkably good diet, much richer in truly good foods than the diet of the ordinary person. And they often report that their diet creates a good feeling, an inner calmness, a happiness that they appear to value even more than the idea that they are protecting animals.

Let's examine the health aspects of vegetarian living and see how a diet without meat can help keep you well nourished, active and healthy.

Are vegetarians well nourished?

There are no grounds to the belief that we need meat in order to be healthy, according to Dr. Jean Mayer, one of America's top nutritionists, Dr. Mark Hegsted, Director of the Human Nutrition Center at the United States Department of Agriculture, and the conservative National Academy of Sciences, which offered the following recommendations in 1974:

Two daily servings of high-protein meat alternates such as legumes, high-protein nuts, peanut butter, meat analogs, dairy products, or eggs are recommended. If dairy products are not used, calcium and riboflavin can be obtained in adequate amounts by liberal intake of dark green, leafy vegetables or by consumption of fortified soy milk. A vegetarian can be well nourished *if* he eats a variety of plant foods and gives attention to the critical nutrients mentioned above.

Rural studies of the Otami Indians in Mexico during the 1950s found that despite a low intake of animal protein, their diet based on tortillas, beans, chili peppers and other local foods was nutritionally sound, while a more recent study by the Virginia Polytechnic Institute showed no protein deficiencies in Appalachian girls whose protein intake was based primarily on cereal grains and legumes. Investigation of the "old people" of Vilcabamba, Ecuador and the Hunzas of Kashmir showed that a plant-oriented diet was not only adequate from a nutritional point of view, but may have played a role in their well-known longevity.

Other nutritional studies in more developed areas agree with the rural studies. During the World War I allied blockade in Denmark the resulting food shortage forced the population to give up meat and consume mostly brown bread, porridge, potatoes, green vegetables and milk. Writing in the *Journal of the American Medical Association*, Dr. Mikkel Hindhede—who conducted the rationing program—reported that mortality figures dropped 17 percent during the first year of rationing. Similar findings were reported in Norway during World War II when consumption of meat was also drastically reduced. Death from circulatory diseases decreased dramatically, but returned to prewar levels when the war was over.

More recent studies in the United States of meat

eaters, lacto-ovo-vegetarians and vegans by Mervyn Hardinge, M.D., of Loma Linda University and Frederick J. Stare, M.D. of Harvard found that vegetarian diets were nutritionally adequate. They found that pure vegetarians partaking strictly of plant foods weighed an average of twenty pounds (9 kilograms) less than the others, who weighed twelve to fifteen pounds above the "ideal" weight. There was no evidence that a lacto-ovo-vegetarian diet was harmful for expectant mothers, nor did a diet without meat affect the growth rates of vegetarian adolescents. The report also found that the corpuscles of the strict vegetarians (vegans) were able to carry more blood than those of the lacto-ovo-vegetarians and the nonvegetarians in the study.

These statistics point out one important fact: as long as we choose from a variety of dry legumes, raw seeds and nuts, whole grains, fresh fruits and vegetables and dairy products (strict vegetarians need a nonanimal source of vitamin B-12 like sea vegetables, miso, or fortified soy milk or brewer's yeast) we will more than meet our daily nutritional needs with a vegetarian diet.

The drug connection

While vegetarian foods are high in protein, vitamins and minerals, they are relatively low in—or entirely free of—cholesterol and animal drugs (such as antibiotics, hormones and tranquilizers) which are given to livestock before slaughter. According to a memorandum prepared by the Director of Veterinary Research of the United States Food and Drug Association, there is a total of nineteen separate animal drugs used in meat-producing animals (including diethylstilbestrol, dinestrol acetate, iponidazole, melengestrol acetate and zeranol) which are suspected of causing cancer. In addition, there are twenty-three separate animal drugs the residues of which could be a human hazard because of "possible supersensitivity, acute toxicity and the development of resistant strains of bacteria." There are sev-

enteen animal drugs that leave toxic residues if not
withdrawn properly, five pesticides which, if abused,
could lead to toxic residues in tissues as a result of
contamination of the environment, and five specialized
drugs which if abused would lead to potent residues
having a possible physiological effect on human beings.

Drug residues in meat wouldn't be such a problem if
the meat inspector would be able to monitor animal
disease and determine levels of hormones, antibiotics
and virulent bacteria in the animal carcass. When I
visited the hog kill floor at a large federally inspected
slaughterhouse in the midwest, I learned that up to
eleven hundred hogs pass before the inspectors every
hour. When I asked an employee what happens if the
inspector happens to find a cancerous tumor, he replied
that the tumor is removed while the remainder of the
animal (which nurtured the malignancy) is passed on for
human consumption.

Pesticides: less of a bad situation

Unless we own a greenhouse or manage our own
organic garden, the presence of at least some pesticide
residues in food is an inescapable fact of life. However,
a vegetarian can make the best of a bad situation. Plant
foods are much lower in pesticide residues than meat
and other animal products. While dairy products generally contain two-fifths the pesticide residues found in
meat (quite a significant reduction in itself) vegetable
fats and leafy vegetables contain only one-seventh as
much. Fruits and legumes contain one-eighth, while
grains and cereals have only one twenty-fourth the pesticide residues found in meat.

Nitrosamines, benzo(a)pyrene and malonaldehyde

Vegetarian foods are also free of dangerous nitrosamines, benzo(a)pyrene and malonaldehyde which are
all suspected carcinogens. Two popular chemicals—

sodium nitrite and sodium nitrate—are well-known additives in the meat industry because they give hot dogs, bologna and other processed meats their fresh red color. Sodium nitrite is a carcinogen. Although sodium nitrate has not been found to be harmful by itself, it can be converted into nitrites through bacterial action in the stomach. The chemical reaction results in the formation of nitrosamines, which have been found to cause cancer.

Benzo(a)pyrene is one of several hydrocarbons which are suspected of stimulating the growth of cancer. An article in *Science* magazine reported that one kilogram (2.2 pounds) of charcoal-broiled steak contains as much benzo(a)pyrene as 600 cigarettes and could contribute to stomach tumors, leukemia and bone cancer.

Still another meat-related chemical not encountered by vegetarians is malonaldehyde, whose existence ordinarily indicates that a food substance is stale or rancid. According to Dr. Raymond J. Shamberger of the respected Cleveland Clinic, malonaldehyde is a carcinogen that can be found in appreciable quantities in beef, poultry, fish and pork. Vegetables and fruits contain little or none of the substance. Dr. Shamberger writes: "The results are consistent with the observation that vegetarians have lower cancer death rates."

Toward a healthy heart

Perhaps one of the best reasons for becoming a vegetarian today is to reduce the risk of hardening of the arteries (atherosclerosis) and heart attack. As early as 1961, the *Journal of the American Medical Association* reported that "a vegetarian diet can prevent 90 percent of our thromboembolic disease and 97 percent of our coronary occlusions."

High levels of cholesterol in the blood have been linked to an increase in heart disease. In 1970, the Inter-Society Commission on Heart Disease Resources (composed of twenty-nine voluntary health agencies including the American Heart Association and the A.M.A.)

identified high fat lipids and high blood pressure as major risk factors in atherosclerosis and recommended the avoidance of egg yolk, bacon, lard and suet with a greater use of grains, fruits, vegetables and legumes in our diets. "It is necessary," the Commission stated, "to encourage further development of high quality vegetable protein products."

These recommendations followed several studies which found that cholesterol and fat levels are substantially lower among vegetarians than among meat eaters. In a study reported in the July 1962 issue of the *American Journal of Clinical Nutrition*, the serum cholesterol levels (in milligrams of cholesterol per millilitre of blood) was 288 for nonvegetarian men and 295 for women, while the lacto-ovo-vegetarians scored 243 and 269 mg/ml respectively. The cholesterol levels of the strict vegetarians were just 206 for both men and women, which represented an overall reduction of 28 percent for men and 30 percent for women. According to the Commission, the risk of developing coronary heart disease among people with a cholesterol level of 250 mg/100 ml of blood or higher is twice that of people with levels under 220 mg/100 ml.

Other investigations tend to support the claim that a vegetarian diet is good for the heart. A recent study in Boston showed that blood pressure levels of vegetarians were more than 20 percent lower than for nonvegetarians, while Dr. Oxfred Müller, the inventor of the capillary microscope found that a vegetarian diet improves blood circulation.

The liver connection

While statistics have shown that meat eaters run a greater risk of fatal heart attack than vegetarians, most doctors are at a loss to explain exactly why heart attacks occur when they do. However some major findings by the Canadian physician William P. Neufeld, M.D. indicate that allergic reactions of the liver to certain foods (especially meat) are a major factor in heart attack.

Although Dr. Neufeld's views weren't made public until he testified before the Senate Select Committee on Nutrition and Human Needs in 1977, many of us have experienced adverse liver reactions to meat when we feel sluggish and bloated after eating it. When toxic substances—such as the bacteria, drugs and other harmful elements found in meat—are encountered by the liver, it tends to swell up to 150 percent its normal size. As the "customs agent" of the body, the liver stops the toxic blood from flowing through the system and works to purify it before permitting it to move on to the heart, brain and other body parts.

In addition to reducing the flow of blood to the heart and brain (which means that these organs receive less life-giving oxygen) the liver's ability to regulate cholesterol can be affected. When repeated allergic reactions occur, cholesterol may be released into the blood by the liver, and accumulate on artery walls. These deposits can lead to atherosclerosis and high blood pressure.

On the day of the heart attack, the victim suffers a strong allergic reaction to the meat-borne toxins. The liver swells up with blood, and the flow of blood to the heart is drastically reduced. Whatever blood flows to the heart is thick and viscid. "When the liver is swollen in an allergic reaction, thus blocking the return flow of blood to the heart, the heart can suffer severe damage," Neufeld told the Committee. The blood tends to clot at its narrowest point and a massive heart attack can result. Most heart attacks occur while we are resting after a meal. Very few occur during strenuous activity.

After nearly fifty years of clinical research, Dr. Neufeld recommends a vegetarian diet to his patients as a way of preventing heart attack. For those who feel they must have meat, Neufeld believes that fresh, and *freshly cooked* unprocessed meats (like chicken or lamb) are best, while reheated chicken, turkey, most fish, beef, cold cuts, sausages and pork products in general produce the worst allergic liver reactions. He also cautions against the use of unripe fruit because it can also produce allergic reactions. However, they are not as severe as those from meat. While still preliminary, Dr. Neufeld's findings can have a radical impact on the prevention and treatment of heart disease, and can help us reduce the risk of heart attack.

The recommendations

Citing the high risk factors of saturated fat, fat in general, obesity and cholesterol in relation to heart disease and stroke, the Senate Select Committee on Nutrition and Human Needs offered the following recommendations in its landmark report *Dietary Goals for the United States* released in February 1977:

1. Increase consumption of fruits and vegetables and whole grains.
2. Decrease consumption of (red) meat and increase consumption of poultry and fish.
3. Decrease consumption of foods high in fat and partially substitute polyunsaturated fat for saturated fat.
4. Substitute nonfat milk for whole milk.
5. Decrease consumption of butterfat, eggs, and other high cholesterol sources.
6. Decrease consumption of sugar and foods high in sugar content.
7. Decrease consumption of salt and foods high in salt content.

The meat packers, the dairy industry, egg producers, cereal manufacturers and the sugar and salt interests were infuriated by the Committee's report, calling its modest recommendations "irresponsible." After an intense lobbying and propaganda campaign (many of the Committee members hailed from the Farm Belt) they forced the Committee to replace its specific recommendations listed above with vague admonitions like "eat a variety of foods," "eat foods with adequate starch and fiber" and "avoid too much sugar."

The controversy surrounding the impact of diet on heart disease is far from over. In the spring of 1980, the Food and Nutrition Board of the National Academy of Sciences—a group generally hostile to vegetarian diets —issued a startling report recommending that healthy Americans need not reduce their intake of cholesterol or saturated fat. While applauded by the National Livestock and Meat Board, the National Dairy Council and the United Egg Producers, it was condemned by the American Heart Association and others who felt that such a recommendation contradicted a wealth of epidemiological evidence which showed that low-fat, low cholesterol diets reduce the risk of heart disease.

The report was followed in January 1981 by release of one of the largest and longest epidemiological studies on diet and heart disease involving over 1900 people over a 23 year period. The study, reported in the *New England Journal of Medicine*, disputed the Board's recommendations, showing that a diet low in cholesterol and saturated fat could reduce the death rate from coronary heart disease by up to 33 percent. According to Richard B. Shekkele, M.D., preventive medicine specialist at Rush-Presbyterian—St. Luke's Medical Center in Chicago, who prepared the final report, "It is prudent to decrease the amount of saturated fats and cholesterol in your diet." His advice is supported by the distinguished nutritionist Dr. Jean Mayer who wrote: "A high serum cholesterol is one of the major risk factors, along with smoking, hypertension and diabetes . . . Certainly there are no iron-clad guarantees that you won't get heart disease . . . But it seems to us only common sense to play the odds."

Cancer

According to the journal *Life and Health*, as much as

80 percent of cancer is now considered preventable. While environmental pollution, heredity and stress are seen as major risk factors in cancer occurrence, smoking and diet alone are believed to account for 90 percent of the preventable potential. After numerous laboratory and clinical studies in the United States and abroad, the evidence shows that a vegetarian diet can reduce the risks of leukemia as well as cancer of the colon, rectum, ovaries and breast. The cancer rates of vegetarians has been found to be roughly half that of the general United States population, while certain cancer rates—such as that for cancer of the colon—are lower still.

High animal fat consumption increases the production of bile acids, which is linked to cancer of the breast, colon and prostate. A major study by Drs. Bantaru S. Reddy and Ernest L. Wynder for the National Cancer Institute showed that Americans consuming a mixed Western diet containing lots of meat produce four to five times more bile acids than vegetarians in the United States, China, and Japan.

The fiber factor

Plant foods—such as legumes, whole grains, fresh fruits and vegetables—are generally rich in dietary fiber, which is recognized as an important factor in cancer prevention. The presence of fiber in the diet reduces the transit time of foods through the gastrointestinal tract by over 50 percent, thus reducing the body's exposure to fecal carcinogens and other toxins. According to the May 1979 issue of *Cancer*, fiber may exert a solvent-like effect and dilute potential carcinogens and help reduce the formation of bile acids in the body. At the Conference on Nutrition in the Causation of Cancer in 1975, Dr. Mark Hegsted outlined a "Prudent Diet" and the risks it would have on the country:

Such diets mean consuming less fat, less meat, less cholesterol, and less food and more fruits, vegetables and cereals, especially crude [whole grain and unrefined] cereals. I believe that the only risk one can identify is to the well-being of the industries [large food refiners, meat packers, etc.] involved. These industries deserve some consideration, but their interests cannot supercede the health interest of the population they must feed.

Other health benefits of vegetarian diets include the prevention and alleviation of gout and a reduced incidence of stomach disorders, diverticulitis, constipation, hemorrhoids, kidney problems and liver disorders. Vegetarian converts have reported improved sleep, greater intuition, a decrease in body odor, and a lighter, cleaner feeling than when they ate meat. One respected Japanese study found that a vegetarian-oriented diet can slow down the aging process.

Physical activity: from jogging to sex

The benefits of vegetarian diets on endurance have been recognized by athletes for years. Murray Rose, the swimming champion who became the youngest triple gold medal winner at the 1956 Olympic Games in Melbourne, is a strict vegetarian, while Johnny Weissmuller set six new swimming records after adopting a vegetarian diet. Before that time, he hadn't broken any swimming records for five years.

Bill Walton achieved his fame as a basketball star without eating as much as a hamburger. Boston Marathon winner Amby Burfoot has frequently testified to the benefits of a vegetarian diet on his running career, while Michael Axinn, the nation's top ranked Junior Marathoner in 1979, claims that his vegetarian diet is essential for his endurance and speed.

Among other achievements, vegetarian Marine Captain Alan M. Jones has lifted a 75-pound barbell 1602 times over his head in 19 hours, skipped rope 100,000 times in 23 hours, and swam half a mile along the frigid

Missouri River one December morning wearing only an athletic supporter.

While most vegetarians don't swim the Missouri River in December, many have reported unexpected benefits they did not enjoy as meat eaters. Some find that a vegetarian diet purifies the body and increases its ability to perceive sights, sounds and other impressions and enhances our capacity to enjoy art, music and dance. Others claim that a vegetarian diet is good for the spirit and increases their ability to meditate and contact their spiritual center. Still others find that a diet without meat enables them to work and play harder during the day, while more sensuous vegetarians report that their diets enhance their ability to enjoy sex when day is done. One vegetarian said: "My vegetarian diet helps me stay trim and sexy. I have more energy, and I don't feel bloated in the evening like I used to be when I ate meat."

Of course, there is no guarantee that a vegetarian diet will save you from cancer, enable you to win a marathon race or transform you into a Don Juan or a Mata Hari. But when we consider the evidence from scientists, medical doctors, nutritionists, athletes and "regular people" from around the world, a vegetarian diet does seem to have much to offer us. In addition to being delicious and inexpensive, it is good for health and pleasure, and will help you achieve your fullest potential as a human being.

SECTION II

How to Take Exquisite Care of Yourself

Chapter 4

VEGETARIAN NUTRITION: THE UNSATURATED FACTS

ALTHOUGH nutritionists point out that even many meat eaters are lacking in essential vitamins and minerals, vegetarians need to pay even closer attention to their food intake.

You don't need a doctorate in applied chemistry to meet your nutritional needs with a vegetarian diet, but it is important to have a general idea of how you can achieve a balanced diet by knowing which foods provide the nutrients that are essential to your well-being.

Nutrition: your number one need

Food consumption alone does not necessarily imply total nutrition, because the air we breathe, our personal habits (such as drinking and smoking), exercise, and our emotional state all play a role in our ability to assimilate nutrients. However this is a book about food, and food plays a decisive role in the healthful upkeep of both mind and body. Briefly stated, we eat for three (and perhaps four) basic reasons:

1. To promote growth, especially during our younger years.

2. To supply fuel needed for the energy used to operate the physical mechanism (the body).

3. To maintain the body structure (bones, tissues, nerves, organs and bloodstream) in top condition and at peak efficiency.

4. For pleasure and enjoyment.

In order to obtain the maximum economic and nutritional value from our food, nutritionists offer the following advice:

Eat quietly and don't rush through your meal. Do not eat when you're emotionally upset, excited, or when tired or in pain. Try to chew food thoroughly, since the first stage of digestion takes place in the mouth. Try to eat only when hungry and avoid eating too much food. Overeating places unnecessary strain on the body, and in addition to making us fat, causes the body to function less efficiently.

Avoid processed, devitalized and chemically treated "foods" such as refined sugar, sweets, white bread and other white flour products, prepared mixed, ready-to-serve products, most commercially prepared cereals and other canned, pickled, preserved or otherwise adulterated food as much as possible. It has been reported that we each consume nearly four pounds of food additives a year in the form of stabilizers, colorings, flavorings, poison sprays, preservatives and emollients. While more needs to be known about the effects of food additives on our health, scientists have found that many are not only unnecessary but harmful. A good rule of thumb regarding food might be: "The less additives the better."

With the increasing use of poisonous sprays on our food supply, many people are considering the value of organically grown products. While many food processors are quick to tell us that organically grown foods have the same nutritional value as food grown with chemical sprays and fertilizers, consumers often feel better about eating fruits, grains and vegetables grown through more natural means.

Raw foods should be eaten whenever possible, especially in the case of vegetables, fruits, seeds and nuts. Although cooking vegetables for twenty minutes or more was popular years ago, nutritionists now note that much of the food value is destroyed through prolonged cooking. The Chinese often lightly sauté or steam their vegetables for a couple of minutes, saving both the flavor and nutritional value.

If foods cannot be purchased fresh, frozen food is better than canned. Frozen food is sometimes even more nutritious than fresh foods, and may be preferable to buy during the winter months. A package of frozen broccoli may have more vitamins and minerals than its "fresh" counterpart languishing on the supermarket vegetable counter.

The plant kingdom is our source of perfect nourishment. Every essential food element necessary for superior nutrition is available from nonmeat sources.

The "RDAs"

RDA is short for "recommended dietary allowance" which is set by the Food and Nutrition Board of the National Academy of Sciences in Washington.

Recommended daily allowances do not serve as an indicator of the adequacy of a given intake for a given individual, because people—and their dietary needs—vary considerably. One person may require only 25 grams of protein a day, while another may need 75. Two people of similar height, weight, age and level of activity may require radically different amounts of vitamin C or iron. Fortunately many of us are attracted to those foods which supply the amount of nutrients our body requires, just like animals in the forest are always attracted to the foods they need in order to survive. One of the advantages of a vegetarian diet is that it purifies the body, and makes it more sensitive to its real nutritional needs.

The recommended allowances provided in this chapter are to serve only as guidelines for the daily intake of those nutrients needed to maintain healthy —meaning disease-free—people. The figures given are for a "normal" man between the ages of 23 and 50 who weighs 154 pounds (70 kilograms) and for a "normal" woman of the same age range who weighs 128 pounds (or 58 kilos). Some people note that in order to provide a margin of safety, the allowances are roughly 20 percent higher than the amounts actually needed. Recommended daily allowances for those living in Canada, the United Kingdom, and Australia are provided for easy reference at the end of this chapter.

THE PROTEIN QUESTION

"So you're a vegetarian. Where do you get your protein?" This is perhaps the most common question asked of people who don't eat meat. Years ago it was taught that meat was the only "good" source of protein, and that without liberal portions of beef, pork and chicken each day, we would suffer from protein deficiency and waste away. Later on, vegetarians were told that the only kind of protein worth eating came from animal sources, and were advised to eat large amounts of eggs and dairy products if they expected to be healthy. After *Diet for a Small Planet* made its debut in 1971, we were told that while plant proteins could be just as good for us as animal proteins, we had to consume them in perfect balance at every meal. While a giant step forward for vegetarianism in general, these recommendations led some people to measure their amino acid intake with a calculator at every meal because they were afraid that they wouldn't be getting enough protein.

Of all the issues surrounding nutrition, protein has been by far the most controversial. Although protein deficiency is extremely rare in this country and most people (including even strict vegetarians) consume twice the protein recommended by the government, new vegetarians are still afraid that their diet won't meet their protein needs.

Protein is of primary importance to each of us. Protein is essential for growth. It regulates the body's water balance and maintains the efficient distribution of body fluids to every cell in the organism. Proteins also serve as buffers which are capable of reacting with either acids or alkalines and prevent any imbalance between the two. In addition, protein is crucial in helping the body combat infection and disease.

Amino acids

Protein is composed of *amino acids*, which are called "the building blocks" of protein. Made up of at least one atom of nitrogen as well as hydrogen, oxygen, carbon and sometimes sulfur, amino acids join together to form a complete protein. There are over twenty different amino acids, and most can be manufactured by the body itself. However, there are nine others which are known as *essential amino acids* because they must be taken through food. Drs. W.C. Rose and Ruth Leverton have reported their findings of the essential amino acids required by adult men and women. The minimum can be fulfilled with about four slices of wholewheat bread and one pint (500 grams) of either cow's milk or soybean milk each day. (See Table 4.1, page 38.)

Proteins: complete and incomplete

A great deal of misunderstanding exists regarding complete and incomplete proteins. A complete protein food is one which contains all of the essential amino acids. According to the United States government publication *Amino Acid Content of Foods*, meat, eggs and dairy products contain all the essential amino acids, but

Table 4.1

DAILY REQUIREMENTS OF ESSENTIAL AMINO ACIDS,
in grams

Amino Acid	Cow's Milk	Soybean Milk	Whole-wheat Bread	Total	RDA Rose (Men)	RDA Leverton (Women)
	(500 grams)	(100 grams)				
Tryptophan	0.245 (0.255)	0.91	0.336 (0.346)	0.25	0.16	
Threonine	0.805 (0.880)	0.282	1.090 (1.162)	0.50	0.31	
Isoleucine	1.115 (0.875)	0.429	1.540 (1.304)	0.70	0.45	
Methionine	0.430 (0.270)	0.142	0.570 (0.412)	1.10	0.55	
Leucine	1.720 (1.525)	0.668	2.340 (2.193)	1.10	0.62	
Cystine	0.155 (0.355)	0.200	0.360 (0.555)	—	—	
Phenylalanine	0.850 (0.975)	0.465	1.320 (1.440)	1.10	0.22	
Valine	1.200 (0.930)	0.435	1.630 (1.365)	0.80	0.65	
Tyrosine	0.890 (0.965)	0.243	1.133 (1.208)	—	0.65	
Lysine	1.360 (1.345)	0.225	1.590 (1.570)	0.80	0.75	

NOTE: Twice the minimum is what Dr. Rose considers an "absolutely safe" intake.

Sources: Orr & Watt; *Amino Acid Content of Foods*
W.C. Rose in *Nutrition Abstract & Review*, No. 27 (1957)
Leverton & Albanese; *Protein and Amino Acid Nutrition*

so do navy, pinto, red and mung beans, garbanzos (chickpeas) lentils, peanuts, soybeans, cornmeal, oats, wholegrain wheat, wheat gluten and brewer's yeast. Some of these foods are very low in one or more of the essential amino acids, and others (termed "incomplete protein foods") may lack one or more altogether. Nevertheless, these foods (like broccoli, many fruits and most nuts) are essential foods just the same. If we choose a food rich in some amino acids and then select a complementary food that supplies us with the other amino acids, we have a complete protein which is equal in value to protein derived from animal sources.

Although the general belief has been that a proper combination of all the essential amino acids must be achieved at each meal, there is strong evidence which indicates that amino acid intake should be considered more on a daily basis instead. According to an article in the *World Review of Nutrition and Dietetics*, protein synthesis is constantly going on in the small intestine and the body utilizes a supply of amino acids all the time and not just three times a day. It has been shown that the body can maintain a balance of the amino acids it gets from food with protein from the body's own "pool" inside the small intestine. This mixture has been found to be relatively constant and serves as a buffer when an amino acid balance is not met from a specific meal. In addition, the intestinal lining is replaced every few days, and its protein is reabsorbed into the body continuously.

As we mentioned before, you don't need a doctorate in chemistry to achieve a proper amino acid balance. This can be readily obtained from any well-chosen vegetarian diet, even if it consists entirely of plant foods. There is no protein problem when we have access to a wide variety of whole grains, legumes, raw nuts and seeds, fresh fruits and vegetables (especially some green leafy ones). Peanut butter makes a good addition, as does a little wheat germ. If you use dairy products and eggs as well, there is certainly no protein problem unless you consume an excess of protein.

Although a combination of the foods listed above will ensure an adequate protein mixture, the combination of certain high protein foods will provide more "protein distance" per meal. Following is a basic listing of those foods which best complement each other, and can be used in hundreds of delicious recipes (see recipe chapter).

rice and legumes	legumes and seeds
rice and soy	rice and dairy products
wholewheat and legumes	cornmeal and beans
sesame and legumes	wholewheat and soy
whole grains and dairy products	

Vegetarian foods which supply high concentrations of protein include soybeans, nuts, whole grains, peanuts, cereals, sunflower and sesame seeds, dried beans and peas, dried brewer's yeast, eggs and cheese.

Table 4.2

PROTEIN CONTENT IN FOOD, 100 grams edible portion

Food	Protein Content (in grams)[a]
Almonds	18.6
Avocados	2.1
Bread, wholewheat, toasted	12.5
Cheese, Swiss	27.5
Chicken, broiled	23.8
Eggs	12.9
Hamburger, broiled	24.2
Knockwurst	14.1
Milk, cow's, fluid	3.5
Milk, soybean, fluid	3.4
Miso	10.5
Peanuts	26.0
Peanut butter	27.8
Peas, dried, split, cooked	8.0
Rice, brown, cooked	2.5
Sesame seeds	18.4
Soybeans, dried	34.1
Soybean flour (low fat)	43.4
Sunflower seeds	24.0
Tempeh	20.0[b]
Tofu	7.8
Wheat germ	26.6
Wheat, wholegrain	14.0
Yeast, dried brewer's	38.8
Yogurt	3.4

Sources: [a]B. K. Watt and A. L. Merrill, *Composition of Foods* (Washington: United States Department of Agriculture, 1963).
        [b]W. Shurtleff and A. Aoyagi. *The Book of Tempeh* (New York. Harper & Row. 1979) p. 33.

Protein deficiency/excess

A deficiency of protein can cause anemia, the inability of the body to resist disease, loss of stamina, muscle deterioration, fatigue and difficulty in healing bruises and wounds. An excessive protein intake over a long period of time is said to possibly aggravate or potentiate certain chronic disease states.

RDA

The recommended dietary allowance for protein has been calculated to be 56 grams for an adult male and 46 grams for an adult female.

CARBOHYDRATES

As opposed to proteins, which are the body-building and repairing elements, carbohydrates provide us with the heat and energy we need in order to function each day.

Sources

The principal sources of carbohydrates include sugar and its products, honey, raisins and other dried fruits, potatoes, cereals, pasta and dried peas and beans. For most people carbohydrates are a major source of calories and a minor source of nutrients. For that reason they fear that if they switch to a vegetarian diet (which is plentiful in carbohydrates) they will have to eat more food and will become fat. However this needn't be the case if we eat the right kinds of carbohydrates. According to Carlton Fredericks in his book *Food Facts and Fallacies*:

> Physiologically, it is best to eat carbohydrates that furnish body-building elements—vitamins, minerals, protein—as well as calories (heat and energy units). This means: eat wholegrain cereals, breads, corn-

meal, barley, buckwheat and rye, and brown rice in preference to white. It also means minimizing the use of white sugar and its products—candy, syrup, sugary drinks, jelly, jam and other stomach filling but body-starving concoctions.

Check out the recipe chapter and find how you can make delicious desserts, shakes and soft drinks that are sugar-free and loaded with nourishment.

RDA

There is no recommended government allowance for carbohydrates because most of us consume far more than is required by the body.

FATS

Fats make up an essential part of a healthy diet. They provide the heat and energy we need daily, and form long-term energy reserves which are stored in various parts of the body. In frigid climates, fat offers protection from the cold. In addition, it protects certain organs of the body—such as the kidneys—from injury.

The planetary consumption of fat varies widely. In the United States we eat so much fat that heart disease and obesity are national epidemics. In places like Mali and Bangladesh, most people have a deficiency of fat, and are therefore highly susceptible to changes in temperature and other factors which threaten their health.

Sources

The principal sources of fat include "visible" fat foods like lard, vegetable oils, butter and margarine. Fat also occurs "invisibly" in foods like meat, cheese, milk, eggs, nuts, peanuts (a legume), seeds and pastry.

Saturated vs. unsaturated

Over the years there has been much controversy

over the issue of saturated fats and unsaturated fats. The basic difference between the two is their chemical composition. Fats are made up of glycerol and fatty acids. The fatty acid part of the fat is composed of a chain of carbon, with each carbon atom having double bonds for the hydrogen atoms to be attached, like the charms on a bracelet. When each carbon atom in the chain has attached to it as many atoms as it can hold (two), it is called a *saturated* fatty acid. When a hydrogen atom is missing from two neighboring carbon atoms, a double bond forms between them and the fatty acid is called *unsaturated*. If there is more than one double bond (i.e. the carbon lacks many hydrogen atoms) the fat is said to be *polyunsaturated.*

Most animal fats are saturated fats, and tend to solidify at room temperature (such as lard). Conversely, most vegetable fats are rich in unsaturated and polyunsaturated fatty acids. Margarine is often advertised as being made from unsaturated oils but the manufacturers don't mention that the oils are changed into margarine by saturating them with hydrogen. For this reason, many vegetarians use liquid oils in their food instead of margarine because liquid oils are far less saturated than margarine and other solid fats.

In his book *Food is Your Best Medicine*, Henry G. Bieler, M.D., stresses the need for only natural, unrefined, and unadulterated fats and encourages the use of vegetable fats found in seeds, nuts, avocados, bananas and other tropical fruits. However he offers the following warning regarding fat in general:

> But fats, saturated or unsaturated, do their greatest harm to the body when they are used as shortening or cooking oil, that is, when they are heated with other foods, especially the starches. Fried bread or potatoes, doughnuts, hot cakes, pie crust, cakes and pastries—all offer altered cholesterol. And when you eat these highly regarded confections, the re-

sult is imperfect artery lining, erosion of the arteries, atherosclerosis. The greater offenders are doughnuts and potato chips, and popcorn a close third (before popcorn will "pop" it must be heated in cooking oil).

Table 4.3

SATURATED AND UNSATURATED FATTY ACIDS
IN FOODS per 100 grams edible portion

Food	Total Grams Saturated Fatty Acids	Total Grams Unsaturated Fatty Acids
Meats		
beef	12	12
lamb	12	9
pork	19	27
Cow's milk	15	10
Soybean milk	3	15
Cheese		
cheddar	18	12
cream	21	13
cottage	2	1
Poultry and eggs		
turkey	4	9
chicken	2	3
chicken eggs	4	6
Fish		
herring (Atlantic)	2	2
tuna	1	1
Separated fats and oils		
butter	46	29
lard	38	56
corn oil	10	81
soybean oil	15	72
safflower oil	8	87
shortening (animal & vegetable)	43	52
shortening (vegetable)	23	72
margarine	18-19	60-61
olive oil	11	83
Cereals and grains		
cornmeal, white	trace	3
millet	1	2
wheat germ	2	8

Food	Total Grams Saturated Fatty Acids	Total Grams Unsaturated Fatty Acids
Fruits and vegetables (including seeds)		
avocado pulp	3	9
olives (mission)	2	16
sesame seed (whole)	7	40
soybeans (dry)	3	13
Nuts and peanuts		
almonds	4	47
Brazil nuts	13	49
coconut	30	2
cashew	8	35
peanut	10	34
pecan	5	59
walnut (black)	4	49

Source: *Composition of Foods*

RDA

There is no recommended daily allowance for dietary fat. At the present time, fats (which are heavily laden with calories) provide 42 percent of the calories in the diet, and many nutritionists would like to see it reduced to 25 or 30 percent.

MINERALS

Minerals are everywhere, and are found in abundance in all vegetarian foods. They include calcium, phosphorus, magnesium, iron and sodium, along with certain trace minerals like iodine and zinc. Nutritionists tell us that if we consume enough of these seven basic minerals, we will be assured of an adequate intake of some twenty others, including cobalt, selenium, chromium, copper and manganese. Our bodies contain some six-and-a-half pounds of minerals, and although we often take them for granted, life would be impossible without them.

Minerals are hard workers, and are indispensable for our proper growth and maintenance. In addition to their body-building functions involving the making of bones, teeth, muscles, nerve tissue, blood, perspiration and stomach tissue, minerals also aid in the digestion of foods and help regulate the temperature of the body.

CALCIUM

What would we look like without calcium? In the first place, we would have a jellyfish-like appearance, because calcium makes up nearly 99 percent of our bones. We would also be without teeth, because calcium makes up nearly 99 percent of those, too. Calcium also helps in the clotting of blood, serves as a catalyst in many biological functions, and regulates the permeability of the cell membrane. In this nuclear age, many people are glad to know (for what it's worth) that calcium regulates the body's intake of Strontium 90, an element contained in radioactive fallout.

Principal sources

Calcium is found in a variety of healthy foods: sesame tahini, wheat germ, kelp and other sea vegetables, cheese, milk, almonds, kale, collards, mustard greens and sunflower seeds.

Certain calcium-rich foods—like spinach, chard, beet greens and parsley—are high in oxalic acid, which reduces our ability to assimilate calcium into our bodies. Phytic acid, normally found in grains used in unleavened bread, can also reduce calcium absorption. For this reason nutritionists suggest that strict vegetarians use leavened bread as a staple in their diets.

Calcium is also affected by our intake of other nutrients. Calcium must be taken in a ratio of 2.5 to 1 of phosphorus, but that is rarely a problem, since most calcium-rich foods are also rich in phosphorus and we often consume both nutrients at the same time. Excessive amounts of protein and fat have been known to decrease the efficiency of calcium utilization by the body, and may be a contributing factor in osteoporosis among older people. Vitamin D also affects calcium absorption, and vitamin D deficiencies can adversely affect our utilization of this important mineral.

Table 4.4

CALCIUM CONTENT IN FOODS, 100 grams edible portion

Food	Calcium Content (in milligrams)
Agar	567
Almonds	234
Blackstrap molasses	684
Bread, wholewheat, toasted	118
Broccoli, cooked	88
Cheese, Swiss	925
Collards, cooked	188
Cornbread, wholegrain	120
Kale, raw	179
Kelp, raw	1093
Milk, cow's (fluid)	118
Milk, soybean (fluid)	21
Mustard greens, raw	183
Peanuts, raw, shelled	69
Rutabagas, cooked	59
Sesame seeds	110
Soybeans, cooked	73
Sunflower seeds	120
Tofu	28
Turnip greens	246
Yeast, dried brewer's	210

Source: *Composition of Foods*

RDA

800 milligrams of calcium are recommended for normal adults.

Deficiency

A calcium deficiency may lead to stunted growth, rickets and convulsions.

PHOSPHORUS

Like calcium, phosphorus is essential for strong bones and teeth, and over 70 percent of this mineral is found in our skeletal structure. Phosphorus is vital to all living and growing tissue, and regulates the release of energy resulting from the "burning" of proteins.

Principal sources

Phosphorus is found mostly in whole grains, nuts, eggs, dairy products, peanuts, legumes, sesame and sunflower seeds, oats, wheat germ, dark green leafy vegetables, meat, root vegetables and dried fruits.

Table 4.5

PHOSPHORUS CONTENT IN FOODS, 100 grams edible portion

Food	*Phosphorus Content (in milligrams)*
Beans, dried, cooked	148
Bread, wholewheat, toasted	302
Brussels sprouts, cooked	72
Cashews	373
Cheese, Swiss	754
Eggs	205
Kale, raw	93
Kelp, dry	240
Lentils, cooked	119
Milk, cow's (fluid)	93
Oats, rolled, raw	405
Peanuts, raw, shelled	401
Prunes, dried	79
Sausage, pork, cooked	162
Sesame seeds, whole	616
Sunflower seeds	837
Wheat germ	1084
Yeast, dried brewer's	1753

Source: *Composition of Foods.*

RDA

The recommended phosphorus intake has been set at 800 milligrams daily for a normal adult.

Deficiency/excess

A deficiency of phosphorus, while unlikely, can lead to general weakness and the demineralization of bones. An excess has been known to lead to the erosion of the jaw or "fossy jaw."

MAGNESIUM

Magnesium is often taken for granted, because nearly everyone gets enough of it in their food. Alcohol is an enemy of magnesium, and many alcoholics have been known to be notoriously low in it. Magnesium works very well with other minerals: like calcium and phosphorus, it is essential for the formation of bones and teeth. Like iron, magnesium is vital for normal body metabolism. It is also a catalyst to help the body utilize calcium and iron efficiently, and helps keep the heart, nerves and muscles in good working order.

Principal sources

The best sources of magnesium happen to be vegetarian foods: nuts, whole grains, legumes, blackstrap molasses, wheat bran, wheat germ and dried brewer's yeast. (See Table 4.6, page 50.)

RDA

The RDA for magnesium is 350 milligrams for a man and 300 for a women.

Deficiency/excess

Magnesium deficiency can lead to growth failure, behavioral disturbances, weakness and spasms, while an excess can bring about diarrhea.

Table 4.6

MAGNESIUM CONTENT IN FOODS, 100 grams edible portion

Food	Magnesium Content (in milligrams)
Almonds, dried	270
Barley, wholegrain	124
Beans, dry, white (raw)	170
Beet greens, raw	106
Cashews	267
Cornmeal, whole ground	106
Hamburger, cooked	21
Lentils, dry	80
Milk, dried skim	143
Millet, whole grain	162
Molasses, blackstrap	258
Oatmeal, dry	144
Peanuts, raw	206
Soybeans, dry	265
Soybean curd (tofu)	111
Spinach, raw	88
Wheat, wholegrain	160
Wheat bran, crude	490
Wheat germ	336
Yeast, dried brewer's	231

Source: *Composition of Foods*

IRON

Iron is the most celebrated of minerals, having been featured on television commercials for years. Our blood supply depends on iron, which helps nourish it with oxygen and promotes the formation of red cells. Iron also helps maintain metabolism and resist disease.

Major sources

Iron can be found in many vegetarian foods: whole seeds, wheat, oats, raisins and other dried fruits, spinach and other leafy greens, dried beans and peas, eggs, brewer's yeast, tofu and certain seaweeds like agar, dulse and kelp.

Table 4.7

IRON CONTENT IN FOODS, 100 grams edible portion

Food	Iron Content (in milligrams)[a]
Agar	6.3
Apricots, dried	5.5
Beet greens, raw	3.3
Blackstrap molasses	16.1
Bread, wholewheat, toasted	2.7
Chard, raw	3.2
Chicken, broiled	1.7
Dates	3.0
Dulse	150.0[b]
Eggs	2.3
Kelp	100.0[b]
Lentils, cooked	2.1
Lima beans, cooked	3.1
Liver, beef, cooked	8.8
Oats, rolled	4.5
Peanuts, raw	2.1
Prune juice	4.1
Raisins	3.5
Soybeans, dry	8.4
Sesame seeds, whole	10.5
Sunflower seeds, raw	7.1
Spinach, cooked	2.2
Tofu	1.9
Walnuts, black	6.0
Wheat germ	9.4
Yeast, dried brewer's	17.3

Sources: [a]*Composition of Foods*
[b]Sharon Ann Rhoads, *Cooking with Sea Vegetables* (Brookline, Autumn Press, 1978)

RDA

18 milligrams for a woman; 10 milligrams for a man.

Deficiency/excess

A deficiency of iron is relatively rare among vegetarians in the United States, but more common in countries like India. Pregnant mothers need lots of extra iron whether they are vegetarians or not, and supplements of 30-60 milligrams are recommended daily. A lack of adequate iron can lead to iron deficiency anemia (which involves general weakness and a reduced resistance to infection) while an excess of iron over a long period of time can lead to siderosis (an excess of iron in the blood or body tissues) and cirrhosis of the liver.

SODIUM

Sodium is often considered to be the least popular of minerals, because many cardiologists recommend low-sodium diets for their patients. Nevertheless, sodium is an essential component in many body fluids, such as blood, tears and perspiration. Although sodium is needed by the body, most of us consume excessive amounts of salt sprinkled on our food. This custom is especially popular with those who have dulled their taste buds after years of eating meat and highly processed foods.

Sources

In addition to table salt, sodium is found in celery, cucumbers, green leafy vegetables, apples, berries, nuts, dairy products (especially cheese) and sea vegetables. Since seaweeds like kelp and dulse (when taken straight from the sea) often contain high amounts of sea salt, nutritionists recommend soaking it in water before adding it to other foods. In general sea salt is preferable to land salt, because it is often rich in trace minerals which the other salt lacks.

RDA

2500 milligrams is recommended for an average adult.

Table 4.8

SODIUM CONTENT IN FOOD, 100 grams edible portion

Food	Sodium Content (in milligrams)
Apples	1
Broccoli, cooked	10
Carrots	47
Celery	126
Cheese, Swiss	710
Collards, raw	43
Cucumbers	6
Currants, black	3
Eggs, poached	271
Grapefruit	1
Kale	75
Milk, cow's (whole)	50
Peanuts	5
Prunes, dried	8-11
Spinach, cooked	50
Seaweed (dulse)	2085

Source: *Composition of Foods*

Deficiency/excess

Most people can easily obtain adequate sodium from their diets even if they use no table salt. However, sodium is lost through heavy perspiration. So if you plan to spend the summer digging ditches in Mississippi or run a marathon through the California desert (or anywhere else) you can become deficient in sodium and suffer from muscle cramps, mental apathy and dehydration. An excessive amount of sodium over a long period of time can lead to high blood pressure.

IODINE

Although it weighs only an ounce or so, the thyroid gland is an extremely important regulator of the body's metabolism. The mineral which is most responsible for the normal action of the thyroid gland is iodine. Iodine also aids in the general growth and development of the body.

Sources

One of the most common sources of iodine in the diet is iodized table salt. However it is also found in eggs, fish and shellfish, dairy products, turnips, spinach and sea vegetables (especially kelp).

Table 4.9

IODINE CONTENT IN FOODS, 100 grams edible portion

Food	Iodine Content (in micrograms)[a]
Vegetables (in general)	28.0
Eggs	14.5
Dairy products	13.9
Breads and cereals	10.5
Fruits	1.8
Kelp	150.0[b]
Dulse	8.0[b]
Kombu	76.2[b]

Source: [a]C.M. Taylor and O.F. Pye, *Foundations of Nutrition* (New York: Macmillan, 1966)
[b]*Cooking With Sea Vegetables*, p. 128.

RDA

150 micrograms of iodine are recommended daily for both men and women.

Deficiency/excess

A deficiency of iodine can lead to goiter (enlarged thyroid) while very high intakes of iodine can depress thyroid activity.

ZINC

Zinc has been largely overlooked (except by Scrabble players) until recently, when nutritionists discovered that it is one of the most important minerals in the body. Zinc is vital for normal growth and sexual development, and aids in the synthesis of proteins and energy. It also promotes carbohydrate metabolism and the healing of wounds.

Table 4.10

ZINC CONTENT IN FOODS, 100 grams edible portion

Food	Zinc Content (in milligrams)
Beans, dry, raw	2.8
Beef, cooked	5.8
Bread, white	0.6
Bread, wholewheat	1.8
Cheese, cheddar	4.0
Eggs, whole	1.0
Granola	2.1
Nuts, Brazil	5.07[a]
Nuts, cashew	4.38[a]
Milk, dry, nonfat	4.5
Oatmeal, dry	3.4
Peanut butter	2.9
Pork loin, cooked	3.1
Wheat, whole	3.4
Wheat bran, crude	9.8
Wheat germ, crude	14.3

Source: "Provisional Tables on the Zinc Content of Foods." In *Journal of the American Dietetic Association*, April, 1975.

[a]"Zinc Content of Selected Food." In *Journal of the American Dietetic Association*, June, 1976.

Principal sources

In addition to meat, zinc can be found in nuts (especially Brazil nuts), whole grains, wheat bran, wheat germ, mature dry legumes, dairy products (especially hard cheese) and eggs.

RDA

The National Academy of Sciences recommends that we consume 15 milligrams of zinc per day, although roughly half that is considered sufficient to achieve zinc equilibrium. The biological availability of zinc in wheat germ is not high. Nuts (especially Brazil nuts) have a very favorable availability of zinc and are considered excellent sources of zinc for vegetarians.

Deficiency/excess

A deficiency of zinc in children can lead to growth failure and small sex glands, while general deficiency symptoms include impaired taste sensation and poor appetite. Although rare, excessive zinc consumption may manifest as fever, nausea, vomiting and diarrhea.

SELENIUM

Called "the most important nutrient to emerge since vitamin E," selenium is a trace mineral found in soils of volcanic origin. While toxic itself in large amounts, selenium protects the body against the toxic effects of heavy metals like cadmium and mercury. It increases the effectiveness of vitamin E, promotes normal sex function, and helps the body fight infectious diseases. After it was found that people who live in areas with rich levels of selenium in the soil have much lower cancer rates than those residing in communities with low soil levels, selenium came to be viewed as an important cancer preventive.

Sources

In addition to meat, selenium is found in garlic, onions, asparagus, mushrooms, eggs, brewer's yeast, wheat and corn.

RDA

There is presently no RDA for selenium, but 50-150 micrograms a day is considered adequate and can be achieved in any well-selected vegetarian diet. A selenium intake of over 350 micrograms is not recommended.

Deficiency/excess

Selenium deficiency can produce anemia. Excessive selenium in the diet has a toxic effect, and can manifest as lung irritation and gastrointestinal disorders.

There are over twenty other trace minerals which are vital for normal body processes. However, there should be no danger of deficiencies in any of these elements as long as we eat a good variety of wholesome foods. If you meet the requirements of the minerals discussed in this chapter, you will meet your minimum needs for the others as well.

VITAMINS

Vitamins are not foods, but make the food we eat usable to the body for proper functioning. Described as a group of food substances which are essential to normal body metabolism, vitamins are present in very small amounts in most foods. However, if they are lacking, a variety of deficiency diseases can result.

Vitamins are classified in two categories: those which are fat soluble and those which are water soluble. The fat-soluble vitamins are easily dissolved in fat, while the water-soluble vitamins can be dissolved in water. This means that foods which contain water-soluble vitamins can lose much of their nutritional value through prolonged soaking or boiling.

VITAMIN A (fat soluble)

Vitamin A is one of our most essential vitamins, yet it is consumed in abundance in most vegetarian diets. Vitamin A promotes growth and general nutrition, prevents night blindness and diseases of the eyes. It is also important for healthy skin, and helps maintain the well-being of the respiratory tract, the throat and the bronchial region.

Sources

Vitamin A is found mostly in carrots, cantaloupe, sweet potatoes, broccoli, squash and other yellow vegetables, spinach and other leafy greens, butter, margarine and fish liver oils.

Table 4.11

VITAMIN A CONTENT IN FOODS, 100 grams edible portion

Food	Vitamin A Content (in International units)	(Retinol Equivalent)
Apricots, dried	10,900	3270
Beet greens, cooked	5,100	1530
Broccoli, cooked	2,500	750
Butter	3,300	990
Cantaloupe	3,400	1020
Carrots, raw	11,000	3300
Eggs, hard-boiled	1,180	354
Spinach, cooked	8,100	2430
Squash, winter, baked	4,200	1260
Sweet potatoes, baked	8,100	2430
Watercress	9,300	2790

Source: *Composition of Foods*

RDA

The National Academy of Sciences recommends 1000 Retinol Equivalents for a male and 800 for a female.

Deficiency/excess

Deficiencies of this vitamin can result in night blindness, changes in the eye, retarded growth, general weakness, hardening of the skin cells, problems of the respiratory tract, genitourinary tract, gastrointestinal tract, nervous tissue and tooth enamel. An excess of vitamin A over a long period can result in headache, vomiting, peeling of skin, severe loss of appetite, and the swelling of long bones. However, large amounts of vitamin A derived from plant sources do not lead to toxic effects, which are most commonly produced by large amounts of concentrated vitamin A supplements.

THE B VITAMINS (water soluble)

The "B" group of vitamins is of tremendous importance. Needed by the body for proper digestion and the efficient use of fuel foods, the B vitamins are also needed to break down proteins so that they can be used effectively by the body. They also aid body growth and help maintain the nervous system in optimum condition.

Nutritionists point out that the B vitamins should be taken in proportionate amounts. For example, a person who consumes a minimum amount of vitamin B-1 should have a proportionate minimum intake of vitamin B-6 in order to prevent deficiencies. This can be met by any well-chosen vegetarian diet, since plant foods are good sources of the B vitamins.

All B vitamins are water soluble, which means that they can lose their potency through prolonged soaking or boiling. In such cases, the soaking or cooking water should be utilized (as broth, for example) so you can obtain the maximum value from foods rich in these vitamins.

VITAMIN B-1 (Thiamin)

Thiamin was first isolated in a laboratory in 1926 when it was found that it was the long-sought-after cure of beri-beri, a nerve disease. While beri-beri is rare in this country today, thiamin performs a variety of other functions: it helps to adjust blood pressure and activate nerves, helps maintain the body's metabolic rate, and aids in the release of energy from carbohydrates.

Main sources

Thiamin is found in a wide variety of foods. In addition to pork and organ meats, thiamin is found in dairy products, wheat germ, whole grains, peas and other legumes, seeds, brown rice, nuts and brewer's yeast.

Table 4.12

THIAMIN CONTENT IN FOODS, 100 grams edible portion

Food	*Thiamin Content (in milligrams)*
Bread, wholewheat	.26
Brazil nuts	.96
Bulgur	.30
Filberts (hazelnuts)	.46
Lentils, cooked	.07
Oats, rolled, (cooked)	.08
Peanuts, raw	1.14
Peas, green, (cooked)	.28
Rice, brown	.09
Soybeans, cooked	.21
Sesame seeds, whole	.98
Sunflower seeds	1.96
Wheat germ	2.01
Wholewheat flour	.66
Yeast, dried brewer's	15.61

Source: *Composition of Foods*

RDA

The RDA for a man is 1.4 milligrams, while that for a woman is 1.0 milligram.

Deficiency

A thiamin deficiency can cause abdominal pains, heart irregularities, muscle tenderness, emotional instability, constipation and irritability. No symptoms of excess have been reported.

VITAMIN B-2 (Riboflavin)

While riboflavin is not as well known as thiamin and niacin, it is very important nevertheless. Riboflavin is closely involved in the energy chain processes of the body, and deficiencies have been linked to increased incidence of cancer and cataract formation.

Major sources

Perhaps the finest source of riboflavin in the diet is dried brewer's yeast, with liver following somewhere

Table 4.13

RIBOFLAVIN CONTENT IN FOODS, 100 grams edible portion

Food	Riboflavin Content (in milligrams)
Almonds	.92
Bread, wholewheat	.15
Cheese, cottage	.25
Eggs	.30
Liver, chicken (cooked)	2.69
Milk, cow's (fluid)	.17
Peanuts, raw	.13
Soybeans, cooked	.09
Spinach, cooked	.14
Steak, porterhouse (cooked)	.16
Sunflower seeds	.23
Wheat germ	.68
Yeast, dried brewer's	4.28

Source: *Composition of Foods*

behind. Good vegetarian sources include wheat germ, leafy vegetables, almonds, whole grains, milk and eggs. Cooking and heat do not harmfully affect the value of riboflavin in foods.

RDA

The National Academy of Science recommends 1.6 milligrams of riboflavin for men and 1.2 milligrams for women daily.

Deficiency

Riboflavin deficiency can manifest in smooth purplish tongue, dry and scaly skin, inflammation of the mouth and lips and retarded growth. Symptoms of excess have not been reported.

VITAMIN B-3 (Niacin)

Like its sister thiamin, niacin is one of the most celebrated of the B vitamins. It plays a major role in the release of energy from carbohydrates, fats and proteins, and aids in the body's general growth. It is also known as the "boosting vitamin" and is often used in large doses to help alleviate depression and other mental illnesses. Niacin also aids in maintaining healthy gums.

Sources

Vegetarian foods are abundant in niacin: brewer's yeast, wheat germ, wheat bran, peanuts, lentils, mushrooms, peanut butter and seeds. Milk and eggs have niacin equivalent.

RDA

The RDA for niacin is 18 milligrams for men and 13 milligrams for women.

Table 4.14

NIACIN CONTENT IN FOODS, 100 grams edible portion

Food	Niacin Content (in milligrams)
Almonds	3.5
Avocados	1.6
Bread, wholewheat (toasted)	3.4
Chicken, roasted	8.8
Lentils, dried	2.0
Lima beans, dried	1.3
Mushrooms, raw	4.2
Peanut butter	15.7
Peanuts	17.2
Peas, green (cooked)	2.3
Potatoes, baked	1.7
Sesame seeds, whole	5.4
Sunflower seeds	5.4
Wheat bran	21.0
Yeast, dried brewer's	37.9

Source: *Composition of Foods*

Deficiency/excess

A deficient intake of niacin can lead to abnormalities in the digestive tract, mental dullness, depression and pellagra. Sometimes niacin can cause temporary symptoms of flushing and a sensation of burning around the neck, face, and hands.

VITAMIN B-6 (Pyridoxine)

The importance of pyridoxine was not known until the 1960s when it made the government's "essential nutrient" list. While it was evident that B-6 helps maintain protein and fatty acid metabolism and the production of antibodies to ward off disease, scientists discovered that pyridoxine helps eliminate edema, particularly before menstrual periods. Others credit B-6 with easing the symptoms of Parkinson's disease, nausea during pregnancy, muscle cramps, sexual disorders, thinning hair and epilepsy.

Basic sources

Pyridoxine can be found in most vegetables, especially cabbage, spinach, potatoes and lima beans, bananas, wheat germ, wholegrain cereals and breads, rice bran, egg yolk and brewer's yeast.

Table 4.15

AVERAGE VITAMIN B-6 CONTENT IN FOODS,
100 grams edible portion

Food	*Vitamin B-6 Content (in micrograms)*
Bananas	300
Cabbage	290
Corn	250-570
Eggs	22
Milk, cow's	65-73
Oats	190-250
Peanuts	300
Peas, split	190-400
Potatoes	160
Spinach	83
Wheat germ	1030-1120
Whole wheat	270-410
Yeast, dried brewer's	3930

Source: *Foundations of Nutrition*, p. 289.

RDA

The recommended allowance for men is 2200 micrograms, while the allowance for women is 2000 micrograms.

Deficiency

A pyridoxine deficiency can lead to mental depression, sore mouth, lips and tongue, insomnia, nervousness, dizziness, nausea and eczema. Symptoms of excess have not been reported.

FOLACIN (Folic Acid)

Folic acid is found in every cell of the body and is necessary for the formation of red blood cells. Like other B vitamins, a lack of folacin has been linked to depression and other mental disturbances, and may be a factor in spontaneous abortion. Folic acid is essential for the formation of RNA and DNA.

Major sources

Folacin is found in dark green leafy vegetables, cauliflower, beans, nuts, fresh oranges, whole wheat, wheat germ and brewer's yeast. It is destroyed by cooking and prolonged storage.

Table 4.16

FOLACIN CONTENT IN FOODS

Food	Folacin Content (in micrograms)
Banana, 1 medium	36
Bread, whole wheat, 1 slice	15-26
Garbanzo beans, ½ cup, dry	125
Lettuce, romaine, 1 cup	102
Oatmeal, quick, ¾ cup, dry	34
Orange juice, 1 cup, fresh	164
Spinach, 4 ounces, fresh	232
Sweet potato, 1 medium	84
Wheat germ, ½ cup	104
Yeast, dried brewer's, 1 tablespoon	308

Source: Laurel Robertson et. al., *Laurel's Kitchen*, (Petaluma CA: Nilgiri Press, 1976).

RDA

The RDA for folacin is 400 micrograms for both men and women.

Deficiency

Folacin deficiency may be a factor in "spontaneous abortion" so pregnant women are urged to consume adequate amounts. In addition, deficiency can lead to anemia, gastrointestinal disturbances, diarrhea and red tongue. Symptoms due to excess folacin have not been reported, although it may help mask any deficiency symptoms of vitamin B-12.

VITAMIN B-12 (Cyanocobalamin)

Next to protein, there is more controversy about B-12 and vegetarian diets than any other nutrient. Although we require tiny amounts of this vitamin, cyanocobalamin is necessary for normal growth and blood formation, and maintains healthy nervous tissue. B-12 also prevents pernicious anemia and improves the biological value of vegetable proteins.

Major sources

The largest amount of vitamin B-12 for most people comes from meat, eggs and dairy products. However there are a variety of sea vegetables and fermented vegetarian foods which contain B-12 as well: Nori, kelp, kombu and wakame are important sources of B-12 from the sea, while miso, tempeh and fortified soybean milk and fortified brewer's yeast are good "land" sources.

It is not really difficult to obtain the necessary amount of B-12. The RDA requirement, low as their standards admittedly are, is only 3 micrograms a day; 2 tablespoons of brewer's yeast provides 4.50 micrograms, and 1½ ounces of kelp 25-50 micrograms, for instance. In any case, vitamin B-12 supplements (derived from yeast sources) can be purchased in any health food store.

Table 4.17

VITAMIN B-12 CONTENT IN FOODS

Food	Vitamin B-12 Content (in micrograms)[a]
Cheese, cheddar, 1 ounce	.28
Cheese, cottage, ½ cup	1.20
Cheese, Swiss, 1 ounce	.50
Egg, 1 large	1.00
Kelp, 1½ ounces	25-50[b]
Kombu, 1½ ounces	25-50[b]
Milk, cow's, 1 cup	1.00
Milk, fortified soy, 1 cup	4.00
Miso, 100 grams	.12[c]
Nori, 1½ ounces	350.00[b]
Tempeh, 100 grams	1.50-3.60[d]
Wakame, 1½ ounces	30.00[b]
Yeast, fortified dried brewer's, 2 tbs.	4.50
Yogurt, 1 cup	.27

Sources: [a]*Laurel's Kitchen*
       [b]*Cooking With Sea Vegetables*
       [c]Shurtleff & Aoyagi, *The Book of Miso* (Brookline: Autumn Press, 1976)
       [d]Shurtleff & Aoyagi, *The Book of Tempeh*

RDA

The National Academy of Sciences recommends that we consume 3 micrograms of vitamin B-12 a day.

Deficiency

Vitamin B-12 deficiency can lead to pernicious anemia. Nutritionists suggest that vegetarians who abstain from eggs and dairy products be especially careful to obtain adequate vitamin B-12. While many vegans take fortified soy milk, fortified brewer's yeast and enjoy sea vegetables in casseroles, soups and salads, some are afraid of not getting enough B-12. Since the vegan diet stresses fresh fruits and vegetables, raw nuts and seeds, legumes, sprouts and whole grains, others believe that such a diet—if eaten on a regular basis—permits the intestine to synthesize its own vitamin B-12, as do the intestines of other vegetarian animals. With the careful use of those foods, there should be no problem about getting enough B-12.

VITAMIN C (Ascorbic Acid) (water-soluble)

Vitamin C: Curer of schizophrenia, reliever of lower back pain, cancer curer, alleviator of carbon monoxide poisoning, reducer of blood cholesterol. Such claims have helped make vitamin C one of the most controversial nutrients of our time. While more clinical research needs to be done to verify such varied claims, it was documented years ago that vitamin C prevents scurvy, hemorrhaging, and diseases of the mouth and gums. It promotes general nutrition, and is seen as a major factor in the prevention of colds. In addition, vitamin C is responsible for the health and maintenance of collagen in the teeth, bones, skin, capillaries and connective tissues, and aids in the detoxification of poisons from the body.

Major sources

Vitamin C is found primarily in fruits and vegetables: citrus fruits, acerola berries, green peppers, tomatoes, broccoli, Brussels sprouts, strawberries, raw cabbage and turnip greens. It is also found in abundance in rose hips, which is taken as a tea or incorporated into vitamin C supplements. It is destroyed by cooking and prolonged exposure to oxygen.

RDA

Because of its importance in human nutrition, the National Academy of Sciences has raised the RDA from 45 milligrams to 60 milligrams for both men and women. (Remember, however, official RDAs do not indicate individual needs and many experts find them far too low. Dr. Linus Pauling, for example, takes 10 *grams* daily.)

Table 4.18

ASCORBIC ACID CONTENT IN FOODS,
100 grams edible portion

Food	*Ascorbic Acid Content (in milligrams)*
Acerola berries	1,300
Broccoli	90
Brussels sprouts	87
Grapefruit	38
Green peppers, raw	128
Lemons	53
Oranges	50
Strawberries	59
Tangerines	31
Tomatoes, raw	23
Turnip greens, cooked	69

Note: Vitamin C is destroyed by drying and cooking. However, less destruction is caused in acid-containing food such as tomatoes.

Source. *Composition of Foods*.

Deficiency/excess

Vitamin C deficiency can lead to scurvy, sores in the mouth, anemia, and the softening of bones and teeth. While considered relatively non-toxic, huge amounts (5000 milligrams a day and over) during long periods of time may lead to the formation of kidney stones. A calcium-potassium supplement can prevent this.

VITAMIN D (fat soluble)

Known to everyone as "The Sunshine Vitamin," vitamin D is manufactured by the skin in the presence of sunlight. Long credited with preventing and curing rickets (a crippling bone-deforming disease of children), vitamin D is essential for growing children and expectant mothers. It promotes the normal calcification of bones and teeth, and for that reason is added to milk during processing.

Sources

Vitamin D is found mainly in fish liver oils, eggs, milk, butter and margarine, as well as direct sunlight.

RDA

Five micrograms of vitamin D are recommended for both men and women. The National Academy of Sciences note that "The requirement for vitamin D can be met entirely by skin irradiation . . ." But some nutritionists recommend between 2,500 and 5,000 I.U. daily; others say 400 I.U. are enough. Since a microgram is one thousandth of a milligram and 1 milligram equals 1 I.U., 5 micrograms is staggeringly low, particularly in the winter time. (I.U.=international units.)

Deficiency/excess

Vitamin D deficiency can lead to rickets (bone deformities) in children, and osteomalacia (a bone disease) in adults. An excess of this vitamin can produce vomiting, diarrhea, loss of weight and possible kidney damage.

VITAMIN E (Tocopherol) (fat soluble)

Perhaps the most acclaimed nutrient since vitamin C, vitamin E is held to prevent and alleviate a wide range of human ills. Because of its ability to prevent the formation of fatty substances and promote blood circulation, researchers like Wilfrid E. Shute, M.D. believe that vitamin E can help prevent and ease the symptoms of heart disease (including angina, rheumatic heart disease and hypertension), stroke and even diabetes. Vitamin E is also an important aid in healing wounds, burns, scars and other skin problems, and helps protect the body's store of vitamins A and D. It helps maintain healthy muscles, and the belief that it helps people remain sexually active has earned vitamin E the title of "the sex vitamin."

Main sources

Vitamin E is found primarily in vegetarian foods. In addition to unrefined vegetable oils, this vitamin can be consumed in wheat germ, whole grain breads and cereals, legumes, green leafy vegetables, eggs, butter and margarine. Strict vegetarians should note that some vitamin E supplements may be in the form of gelatin capsules. (See Table 4.19, page 72.)

RDA

The RDA for vitamin E is now measured by the government in milligrams of tocopherol equivalents and is set as 10 for men and 8 for women. One milligram of natural vitamin E = 1.49 I.U. (Dr. Wilfrid Shute recommends 1200 I.U.—International Units—daily.)

Deficiency

Although rare, a deficiency can manifest as anemia. Since vitamin E is relatively nontoxic, symptoms of excessive use have not been reported.

There are a number of other important vitamins including vitamin K and several B vitamins like pantothenic acid, biotin and choline. While these elements are recognized as essential to human nutrition, it is believed that if the requirements for the other vitamins are met, the necessary amounts for these elements will be achieved as well. Vegetarians as well as non-vegetarians can balance their nutritional requirements with supplements as needed from their health foods store.

Table 4.19

FOOD CONTAINING THE LARGEST AMOUNT OF VITAMIN E

Food	Vitamin E(mg)
Apples	.74 in one medium apple
Bacon	.53 in about 10 slices, broiled
Bananas	.40 in one medium banana
Navy beans, dry	3.60 in ½ cup, steamed
Beef steak	.63 in 1 piece steak
Butter	2.40 in 6 tablespoons
Carrots	.45 in 1 cup
Celery	.49 in 1 cup
Cornmeal, yellow	1.70 in about ½ cup
Corn oil	87.00 in about 6 tablespoons (14.5 in 1 tablespoon)
Eggs, whole	1.00 in one whole egg
Grapefruit	.52 in about ½ grapefruit
Lettuce	.50 in 6 large leaves
Oatmeal	2.10 in about ½ cup cooked oatmeal
Peas, green	2.10 in 1 cup peas
Potatoes, sweet	4.00 in 1 small potato
Rice, brown	2.40 in about ¾ cup cooked
Soybean oil	140.00 in 6 tablespoons (23.33 in 1 tablespoon)
Turnip greens	2.30 in ½ cup steamed
Wheat germ oil, medicinal	320.00 in 6 tablespoons

Source: Reprinted from *Complete Book of Vitamins* © 1966 by Rodale Press, Inc. Permission granted by Rodale Press, Inc. Emmaus, PA 18049.

NUTRITIONAL SUPPLEMENTS?

While all doctors, nutritionists and other health experts recognize our need for a well-balanced diet designed to satisfy the government's recommended daily allowances, they differ on the subject of food supplements. The more conservative experts (including many medical doctors) believe that we can satisfy all our nutritional needs through diet alone, while those on the opposite extreme suggest that we consume enormous quantities of literally dozens of vitamin and mineral supplements every day in order to stay healthy. As a result, the consumer is often confused and nutrition can become a hit-and-miss affair. Whether you are a vegetarian or a meat eater, the controversy over supplements is important to you and your family.

In its ideal state, our food would be able to provide us with an abundance of nourishment: peas would be picked fresh from the garden and eaten soon thereafter, while oranges would be plucked from the tree and enjoyed as fruit or juice at the peak of ripeness. Nuts would be shelled and immediately eaten, while grains would be stoneground and eaten within the week.

While some people still grind their own flour and eat their vegetables fresh from the garden, most of us do not. Our food is often transported from across the country (and from around the world) and may have lost some essential nutrients during the long journey and during storage. In addition, food may be grown in soil which is deficient in certain minerals, while modern food refining and processing can destroy certain nutrients which were originally part of the food in its natural state.

For these reasons, health educators often recommend that we take daily nutritional supplements to provide a margin of safety against deficiencies. Some suggest that vitamin and minerals in the form of pills are best, while experts like Dr. Paavo Airola prefer high power foods such as brewer's yeast, raw wheat germ, rose hips, kelp, lecithin and whey powder which often provide essential micronutrients which may not have yet been discovered by scientists.

For individuals who require a therapeutic vitamin and mineral program (which should be done with the guidance of a qualified specialist) Airola suggests that large amounts of vitamin C, vitamin E, vitamin A and vitamin B-complex be taken with meals. The key to healthy nutrition is to avoid extremes.

Many vegetarians find that after several months on a

meatless diet their bodies are more sensitive because they are cleansing themselves of the drugs, pesticide residues and bacteria found in meat. As a result, they are often more aware of an inner intelligence of bodily needs.

If you decide to use nutritional supplements, use those which are natural rather than synthetic as much as possible. While synthetic vitamins and minerals may provide adequate amounts of certain nutrients, they may be lacking in trace elements which are often found in supplements derived from natural sources.

There are many books on nutrition. A selective listing can be found in Appendix C.

Table 4.20

RECOMMENDED DAILY DIETARY ALLOWANCES

	Canada[a]		United Kingdom[b]		Australia[c]	
Sex	M	F	M	F	M	F
Age	25	25	18-35	18-35	25	25
Weight (kg)	72	57	65	55	70	58
Activity	moderate		moderately active		moderate	
Calories (kcal)	2850	2400	3000	2200	2900	2100
Protein (gm)	50	39	75	55	70	58
Calcium (mg)	500	500	500	500	400-800	400-800
Iron (mg)	6	10	10	12	10	10
Vitamin A (IU)	3700	3700	3750	3750	2500	2500
Thiamin (mg)	0.9	0.7	1.2	0.9	1.2	0.8
Riboflavin (mg)	1.4	1.2	1.7	1.3	1.5	1.1
Niacin equiv. (mg)	9.0	7.0	18.0	15.0	18.0	14.0
Vitamin C (mg)	30.0	30.0	30.0	30.0	30.0	30.0

Sources: "Recommended Daily Intakes of Nutrients Adequate for the Maintenance of Health Among the Majority of Canadians," *Canadian Bulletin of Nutrition*, 6, 1, 1964.

"Recommended Daily Intakes of Energy and Nutrients for the UK," Department of Health and Social Security, London, 1969.

"Dietary Allowances for Australians," In *Medical Journal of Australia*, Vol. 1, June 11, 1965, p. 1041.

Chapter 5

MENU PLANS FOR VEGETARIANS: LACTO-OVOS AND VEGANS

MANY people have questions about what to eat as vegetarians, and fear that they would have to give up eating pleasure if they gave up steak and roast beef from their diets. One friend pointed out that he saw little need to live a long life if didn't get any pleasure from his food, while another was afraid that all she could eat as a vegetarian would be beans, potatoes and salads. Their fears are valid and important, and are a challenge to health-minded gourmets everywhere.

With a little imagination and a touch of derring-do, a healthy vegetarian diet can be a pleasure to eat, will go easy on your food budget, and will save you time in the kitchen.

What does this diet consist of? Generally speaking, if we choose daily from a wide variety of whole grains, dried legumes, whole seeds, nuts, sprouts, fresh fruits and vegetables along with some dairy products and perhaps eggs, we will not only be assured an abundance of protein, but a good supply of essential vitamins and minerals as well. And, these foods can be prepared in a variety of ways that will impress the most choosy gour-

met. While we'll review specific menu plans for strict
vegetarians (vegans), lacto vegetarians, pregnant women,
young children, people who want to lose weight, and
athletes in this and the next two chapters, the following
eight-point program can help you discover the pleasures of creative vegetarian cuisine. In addition, it will
help you save money on food and yet provide more
than enough of the nutrients you need to be healthy.

1. *Take a world tour.* Most basic foods like whole
   grains, rice, beans and fresh vegetables form the
   staple ingredients of some of the world's most exciting dishes. Try your hand at Greek *spanikopitas*
   made from fresh spinach and feta cheese. Or prepare an exciting Indian curry for under fifty cents a
   serving. Middle Eastern delights like *hummus*—made
   with garbanzo beans and sesame tahini, garlic and
   lemon juice—take only a few minutes to prepare and
   when eaten on pita bread, have as much protein as
   hamburger. Mexican tacos, chilis rellenos, stir-fried
   Oriental vegetables, Yankee bean soup and wholewheat Italian pasta dishes are a few of the hundreds
   of nutritious and exciting ethnic dishes you can choose
   from. Dozens more are included in the recipe section of this book.
2. *Choose a variety from one basic food type.* Beans,
   for example, come in dozens of varieties and each
   kind imparts a unique flavor, color and texture. Some,
   like garbanzos, are good in spreads and casseroles.
   Others, like cowpeas and black beans, are terrific in
   soup. Mung beans and lentils are good for sprouting,
   while red beans and kidney beans are best in chili,
   bean paté and salads. Experience the pleasures of a
   variety of legumes, grains and green vegetables!
3. *Spark up your salad.* Most salads are so dull, there
   is little wonder why so many people can't stand
   them. Visit your local greengrocer and create a dis-
   tinctive salad with Chinese cabbage, kale, leeks,

watercress, spinach greens and crisp romaine. To this basic foundation (you needn't use all these greens at once) add a handful of fresh sliced mushrooms, cherry tomatoes, alfalfa sprouts and sunflower seeds. Top your salad with a fresh homemade dressing. Mix vinegar, oil, lemon juice, tahini, soy sauce and a touch of garlic and you have an excellent three-minute dressing that costs less than commercial dressings. Stock your pantry with oregano, dill, thyme, cumin and mustard and use these basic spices to add zest to your meals.

4. *Indulge your palate.* As you liberate your protein bill from expensive items like meat by buying cheaper proteins (like beans, grains and rice) you'll have more money to spend on those healthy but costly goodies you've always enjoyed. Add a few dried Oriental mushrooms to your soup. Top your salad with avocado slivers, hearts of palm, or marinated artichoke hearts. Buy yourself an exotic melon and enjoy a slice for a midnight snack. Even with such occasional indulgences, you'll still save money on food and you'll enjoy the kind of pleasure that won't hurt your health.

5. *Be artistic!* Fresh vegetables and fruits are beautiful and lend themselves to a variety of creative artistic designs.

6. *Experiment!* Try some of the "new" foods that have been rapidly gaining favor among adventurous food lovers. Tofu—soy bean cheese—is found in most Oriental groceries and natural food stores. Tahini, kudzo, bancha tea, tempeh, tabouli, miso and kombu are some of the foods that can add a touch of exotica to our meals.

7. *Save yourself time.* What good is a pleasant meal if you are too tired to enjoy it? On a given morning, cook up several kinds of legumes and freeze them for future use. Make them into vege-burgers, soups, dips, casseroles and paté later on. If the basics are

ready to go, your gourmet meal can be ready in
thirty minutes or less.

8. *Invest in a few good vegetarian cookbooks.* A good
cookbook can open up new horizons in good eating,
can save you time in the kitchen, and perhaps save
you money as well. Consult the listing of some of the
best vegetarian cookbooks in The Vegetarian Book-
shelf at the end of this book.

Meal plans for lacto-ovo-vegetarians

Being a lacto-ovo-vegetarian is only slightly less con-
venient than being a meat-eater (soybean burgers aren't
quite as popular as Big Macs just yet) but generally
easier than being a pure vegetarian or vegan. While the
strictly vegan diet isn't all that difficult to maintain,
vegans need to pay more attention to their daily intake
of protein, calcium and B vitamins (especially vitamin
B-12) than those who consume milk and eggs.

Since a lacto-ovo-vegetarian diet can contain any food
except red meat, poultry and fish, it is no surprise why
most vegetarians choose this diet for convenience and
nutritional security. The only problem with this kind of
diet is that it can be abused. A lacto-ovo-vegetarian can
easily fill up with white flour products, thick gravies
and sauces, ice cream and frosted cakes, and other
foods which are high in calories, sugar, saturated fat
and low on fiber and essential nutrients.

For that reason, we have devised "The Daily Vegeplan"
as a basic vegetarian food guide. It is unlike the traditional Four Food Groups which places heavy emphasis
on meat and dairy products and gives no guidance
about fresh and whole foods. The Daily Vegeplan is
based on the recommendations of the Senate Select
Committee on Nutrition and Human Needs. While it is
high in fiber, high in nutrients and stresses natural,
unprocessed foods, the Vegeplan recommendations are

low in fat, calories, sugar and salt. When used in a creative way, your Daily Vegeplan will be both healthy and delicious.

DAILY VEGEPLAN FOR
LACTO-OVO-VEGETARIAN ADULTS

Protein Group: Three daily servings of the following: mature legumes, nuts or seeds, commercially prepared or homemade protein mixtures (gluten, soyameat, tempeh, nutmeats, cereal-legume-nut combinations), low-fat milk and dairy products and eggs.

This group provides mainly protein, B vitamins, fat, minerals (especially iron) and other micronutrients. Plant proteins supply abundant fiber as well, a component found lacking in most American diets.

Vegetable Group: Three or more liberal servings daily of: fresh dark green and yellow vegetables, leafy greens, sprouts and other vegetables including carrots, onions, radishes and tomatoes (though technically a fruit).

This group supplies mainly vitamins A, B, C, cellulose, fiber, iron, calcium and trace minerals.

The Fruit Group: Three or more liberal servings of: fresh fruits and their juices, with special attention given to sources of vitamins A and C.

This category provides primarily minerals and vitamins A and C, as well as dietary fiber.

The Energy-Fiber Group: At least four servings daily: including brown rice, wholegrain breads and cereals. Potatoes and other starchy vegetables would be included.

This group provides mostly carbohydrates, protein, B vitamins, and natural dietary fiber.

THE SEVEN DAY
LACTO-OVO-VEGETARIAN PLAN

The following week-long menu plan was designed especially for lacto-ovo-vegetarians and is based on the daily vegeplan described above. Dishes marked with an asterisk (*) are from recipes you can find in the recipe section of this book.

DAY 1

BREAKFAST *Bircher muesli with low-fat milk
Fresh apples, peaches or strawberries
Herb tea, juice or coffee substitute

LUNCH *Chickpea corn soup
*Gazebo sandwich with cottage cheese
Baked apple with cinnamon
Milk or fruit shake

DINNER *Peppers stuffed with beans
Zucchini with tomatoes
2 slices of wholegrain bread with butter
Mineral water with a slice of lime

DAY 2

BREAKFAST Low-fat yogurt with fruit, nuts and wheat germ
2 slices wholegrain toast with sugarless preserves
Herb tea or coffee substitute

LUNCH *Luxembourg navy bean soup
Cottage cheese salad
Fresh fruit

DINNER *Cashew nuts and raisin pulao
Broccoli
Halvah
*Fruit soda, homemade

DAY 3

BREAKFAST Orange juice (fresh or frozen)
*Crunchy granola with low-fat milk
¼ cup raisins
Sliced pears

LUNCH *Soybean burgers with cheese

              Avocado sprout salad with tomatoes
              Wholewheat rolls (for the burger)
              Milk or shake
DINNER   *Walnut almond loaf
              Spinach or kale
              Grated carrot salad with raisins
              Fruit salad with *Freya's topping or whipped
                cream

DAY 4

BREAKFAST Half grapefruit
              Oatmeal (⅔ cup, dry) with low-fat milk
              ¼ cup raisins
              Milk or herb tea
LUNCH   *Hummus on pita bread
              Parsley and tomato salad with herb dressing
              Apple juice
              Banana
DINNER   *Lima bean soup
              Sprout salad
              Scandinavian flatbread with cheese
              Strawberries and cream

DAY 5

BREAKFAST Pineapple juice (unsweetened)
              Western omelette (without ham)
              Stewed apricots
              Wholegrain toast with butter or margarine
              Milk
LUNCH   *Ahimsa pea soup
              Swiss cheese sandwich with alfalfa sprouts on
                2 slices wholegrain bread
              Strawberry milkshake with honey
DINNER   Vegetable tacos with cheese
              Corn on the cob
              Tossed salad
              Milk or tea
              Ice cream

DAY 6

BREAKFAST Orange juice (fresh or frozen)

             Cooked bulgur with dates, honey and milk
             Fresh pear slices
             Milk, tea, or coffee substitute
LUNCH   *Llapingachos (Ecuadorian potato pancakes)
             Steamed broccoli or zucchini
             Cucumber-lettuce salad with mushrooms and
                 dressing
             *Strawberry smoothie
DINNER   *Japanese moyashi
             Brown rice
             Steamed kale
             Tea
             Ice cream or fresh fruit salad

DAY 7

BREAKFAST   One orange
            French toast (2 slices) with honey, maple syrup,
                or sugarless preserves
            Low-fat milk
LUNCH   *Tomato-lentil-rice soup
            Toasted wholewheat English muffins topped
                with cheese and sprouts
            Pineapple-apple drink
DINNER   *Lou Ann's Special Spaghetti Dinner
            Vegetable antipasto
            Wholewheat bread with butter or margarine
            Fresh fruit salad

Meal plans for vegans

My personal experience with a vegan diet led me to
explore many new foods and recipe ideas which I probably wouldn't have encountered as a lacto-ovo vegetarian. I soon discovered that with a little imagination I was
able to choose from a broad spectrum of healthy foods
which satisfied my daily need for protein, minerals and
vitamins (especially vitamin B-12).

A basic vegan food plan can be based on the Daily
Vegeplan described earlier. When adapted for vegan
diets, the vegeplan looks like this:

DAILY VEGEPLAN FOR VEGAN ADULTS

Protein Group: Three daily servings of:
 mature legumes, tofu, nuts and seeds (approximately ½ cup), commercially prepared or homemade protein mixtures (gluten, soyameat, tempeh, nutmeat, cereal-legume-nut combinations).

Vegetable Group: Three or more liberal servings daily of:
 fresh dark green and yellow vegetables, leafy greens, sea vegetables (kelp, dulse, kombu, nori), sprouts and other vegetables including carrots, onions, radishes and tomatoes. Eat at least one raw salad every day, and choose vegetables as a snack food instead of cookies, candy, nuts and other high-calorie foods.

Fruit Group: Three or more liberal servings of:
 fresh fruits and juices, with special attention given to sources of vitamins A and C.

Energy-Fiber Group: At least four servings daily of:
 brown rice, wholegrain breads and cereals. Potatoes and other starchy vegetables would be included in this group.

Nutritionists suggest that a vegan can be healthy as long as he or she receives an adequate amount of vitamin B-12, which is found primarily in foods of animal origin. However, vitamin B-12 is also found in seaweed, miso, tempeh, fortified soybean milk and fortified brewer's yeast as well as in available supplements.

THE SEVEN DAY VEGAN GOURMET DIET PLAN

The following seven vegan daily menus are based on the belief that eating for health can indeed be eating for pleasure. The following easy-to-prepare menus are designed to provide your basic nutritional needs without burning a hole in your food budget.

DAY 1

BREAKFAST One orange
Cooked oatmeal (⅔ cup dry) with maple syrup
¼ cup raisins
Wholewheat bread (2 slices) with sugarless
    preserves
Herb tea or coffee substitute

LUNCH *Lentil burgers (2) on wholegrain bread or rolls
Baked potato with margarine or other oil
1 cup cooked broccoli
1 sliced tomato
Sprouts for the burger
*Fresh fruit smoothie (*see* Strawberry smoothie)

DINNER *Pasta e Fagioli
1 cup cooked kale
Fig/apple/apricot salad
Mineral water with a slice of lime

Analysis of typical meal, dinner above

	CAL	FAT gm	PRO gm	CA mg	FE mg	B1 mg	B2 mg	B3 mg	Vit.A RE/eq.
	2955	93	94	1412	36.5	3.0	2.1	32	9376
RDA (1980)	—	—	56	800	10.0	1.2	1.6	19	1000 (Men)
	—	—	44	800	18.0	1.1	1.3	14	800 (Women)

DAY 2

BREAKFAST 1 cup orange juice (fresh or frozen)
*Wholewheat pancakes with raisins (six)
Maple syrup or sugarless preserves
1 fresh apple or banana
Herb tea or coffee substitute

LUNCH *Gazebo sandwich on wholewheat pita bread
Chilled apple juice
*Strawberry vegan ice cream

DINNER *Ahimsa pea soup
*Oatcakes with vegetables Archambault
Tossed green salad with sprouts and herb dressing
*Dried fruit drink
Herb tea

DAY 3

BREAKFAST Half grapefruit
　　　　　　*Bircher muesli
　　　　　　Fresh apples, peaches or strawberries
　　　　　　Soybean milk
　　　　　　Herb tea or coffee substitute
LUNCH　　　*Lima bean soup
　　　　　　*Hummus on wholegrain toast
　　　　　　Shredded cabbage/carrot salad with herb
　　　　　　　dressing
　　　　　　Fresh carrot juice
DINNER　　*Tofu-vegetable supreme
　　　　　　Wholewheat noodles
　　　　　　Sliced cucumber and tomato salad
　　　　　　Fresh fruit with *Freya's topping

DAY 4

BREAKFAST Apple juice
　　　　　　*Scrambled tofu
　　　　　　Wholewheat toast (2 slices) with margarine
　　　　　　Herb tea
LUNCH　　　*Oriental lentils with brown rice
　　　　　　Tomatoes and parsley with herb dressing
　　　　　　*Carobanana shake
　　　　　　Citrus salad with *Freya's topping
DINNER　　*Lou Ann's Eggplant Dinner
　　　　　　Corn on the cob
　　　　　　Tossed salad with sprouts
　　　　　　Wholegrain rolls
　　　　　　*Fruit-nut loaf

DAY 5

BREAKFAST Wholewheat cooked cereal (⅔ cup dry)
　　　　　　Diced dried apricots, raisins or prunes
　　　　　　Wholegrain toast (2 slices) with sugarless jelly
　　　　　　One banana
　　　　　　Herb tea
LUNCH　　　*Hearty vegetarian vegetable soup
　　　　　　*Beanpot with oregano over rice
　　　　　　Coleslaw (without mayonnaise)
　　　　　　Cornbread (2 slices)

                    *Pineapple delight
DINNER   *Stuffed peppers
                    Baked potato
                    Zucchini with tomatoes
                    Fruit salad with raisins and dates
                    Mineral water with a slice of lime

DAY 6
BREAKFAST Fresh grapefruit juice
                    Corn grits (¾ cup, dry) sweetened with maple
                        syrup or honey
                    ¼ cup mixed raisins and sunflower seeds
                    Sliced pears
LUNCH   *Tempeh in tomato sauce
                    Sprout salad with French dressing
                    Wholegrain bread (2 slices)
                    *Strawberry smoothie
DINNER   *Curried chickpea dinner
                    1 cup steamed Brussels sprouts
                    Raisins and cashew pieces as curry garnish
                    Tea

DAY 7
BREAKFAST *Crunchy granola with fresh fruit
                    Soybean milk or apple juice for cereal
                    Herb tea or coffee substitute
LUNCH   *Tahini-noodle soup
                    *Salvadorean baked rice
                    Wholegrain corn chips or tacos
                    *Fruit smoothie (*see* Strawberry smoothie)
DINNER   *Tofu in black bean sauce
                    Brown rice
                    Alfalfa sprout salad
                    *Strawberry orange flip
                    *Carob banana vegan ice cream

Chapter 6

SPECIAL MENU NEEDS: PREGNANT WOMEN AND CHILDREN

Diets during pregnancy

A lacto-ovo-vegetarian diet is adequate for both pregnant women and lactating mothers. While exhaustive studies have not been done with vegan mothers, a vegan diet can be equally suitable as long as the mother-to-be takes extra care to obtain adequate nutrients.

According to the Recommended Dietary Allowances published in 1980 by the Food and Nutrition Board of the National Academy of Sciences, pregnant women need to increase their intake of all the recommended nutrients with special attention given to protein, vitamin D, vitamin B-2 (riboflavin), calcium, iron and folacin. All are easily obtainable on a diet without meat even if the mother-to-be eats only plant foods.

In addition to the fact that vegetarian diets contain less toxins and are free from most (or all) animal drug residues found in meat-oriented diets, pregnant vegetarians discover that the high fiber content of a vegetarian diet enables them to eliminate body toxins more easily and keeps them more resistant to disease.

Another major consideration is folic acid, a B vitamin often found lacking in meat-eating pregnant women. Found primarily in raw vegetables and fruits (it is especially vulnerable to cooking), folic acid deficiency symptoms include anemia, fatigue and lowered resistance to disease. Since vegetarians normally consume far more folic acid than the average meat eater, this serious problem among pregnant women is virtually eliminated for vegetarians.

Nevertheless, a woman's diet during pregnancy is not an issue to be taken lightly. The following diet plan (adapted in part from *Birth and the Family Journal* and *Laurel's Kitchen*) is designed to provide the basis for a sound vegetarian diet during pregnancy.

DAILY VEGEPLAN FOR PREGNANT WOMEN

Protein Group

> *Lacto-ovo-vegetarian*: Four daily servings of:
>> mature legumes, nuts and seeds, commercially prepared or homemade protein mixtures, low-fat dairy products and eggs.
>
> *Vegan*: Same as above, without the dairy products and eggs. Use instead three cups of calcium or B-12 fortified soy milk or a nutritional supplement high in vitamin B-12, calcium and iron.

Vegetable Group

> *Lacto-ovo-vegetarian*: Three or more liberal servings daily of:
>> fresh dark green and yellow vegetables, leafy greens, sprouts and other vegetables, including carrots, onions, radishes and tomatoes.
>
> *Vegan*: Four or more liberal servings of the above.

Fruit Group

> *Lacto-ovo-vegetarian*: Three or more liberal servings of:
>> fresh fruits and juices, with special attention given to sources of vitamins A and C.
>
> *Vegan*: Same as above.

Energy-Fiber Group

> *Lacto-ovo-vegetarian*: At least three servings daily: including brown rice, yeast-raised wholegrain bread (2 slices = 1 serving) and cereals.
>> Include at least óne serving of potato or other root vegetable such as turnips or yams.
>
> *Vegan*: Four liberal servings of the above.

What would a typical daily menu be like? While some nutritionists treat a pregnant women like a patient suffering from a disease, thousands of pregnant vegetarians are discovering that a highly nutritious diet needn't be at all dull.

THE THREE DAY PREGNANCY DIET PLAN

DAY 1

BREAKFAST	¾ cup unsweetened pineapple juice
	Six small wholegrain pancakes fried in 1-½ tablespoon oil with 2 teaspoons margarine and 1 teaspoon of molasses or maple syrup
	10 medium stewed prunes
	Herb tea or coffee substitute
SNACK	1 cup chilled apple juice
LUNCH	Peanut butter and banana sandwich on wholegrain bread (3 tablespoons peanut butter and ½ banana)
	¾ cup collard greens, steamed
	½ cup fresh strawberries
	Beverage

SNACK   Carrot sticks (1 carrot)
DINNER   *Ahimsa pea soup over
                 ½ cup cooked brown rice
              1 slice wholewheat bread
              Fresh pears
              Herb tea

Analysis of typical meal, dinner above

	CAL	FAT gr	PRO gr	CA mg	FE mg	B1 mg	B2 mg	B3 mg	A RE/eq.
	3062	121	82	1205	21.4	2.0	1.64	40.7	10,303
RDA (1980)	2200	—	65	1200	18.0*	1.1	1.80	15	2,000

*In addition, daily iron supplements of 30-60 mg. are recommended for all pregnant women.

DAY 2

BREAKFAST Half grapefruit
           2 slices wholewheat toast with 1 teaspoon
              margarine
           Corn grits, enriched (¾ cup dry) with
              ½ cup raisins, 1 tablespoon molasses and ⅓
              cup milk or fortified soy milk
           1 peach
           1 cup skim milk or fortified soymilk
SNACK   20 roasted peanuts and 18 cashews
LUNCH   *Chickpea-vegetable casserole, 2 servings
           Wholewheat noodles, 1 serving
           Mustard greens, cooked
           Carrot sticks, from 1 carrot
           1 slice wholegrain bread
           *Fruit smoothie (*see* Strawberry smoothie)
DINNER   *Vegetarian chili
           1 cup cooked broccoli
           cucumber and tomato salad
           2 slices wholegrain bread
           1 medium banana
           *Grape soda (*see* Fruit soda)

DAY 3

BREAKFAST	*Bircher Muesli with raisins and milk
	1 slice wholegrain toast with margarine
	Sliced pears
	1 cup skim milk or fortified soy
SNACK	1 cup tomato juice and celery sticks
LUNCH	*Chickpea-corn soup
	*Tabouli salad on wholewheat pita bread
	*Carobanana shake (with milk or fortified soy)
DINNER	*Paella vegetariana
	Broccoli
	1 slice wholewheat bread
	Parsley-tomato salad with tahini dressing
	*Strawberry orange flip
	Diced apples with *Freya's dressing

Should you take supplements?

Supplements should not be a substitute for the kind of nutritious daily diets outlined on the preceding pages. However, mothers-to-be are more secure with the extra margin of safety that nutritional supplements provide. As with all nutritional supplements, make sure that they supply you with the kinds of nutrients you need especially during pregnancy, such as iron, riboflavin, calcium and vitamin D.

Finally: some general advice

Avoid dieting, fasting, drugs, coffee and alcohol as much as possible, and try to eliminate as many "empty calorie foods" as much as possible. If you are well nourished with a good vegetarian diet when you become pregnant, and continue to eat well during pregnancy, you will join the thousands of vegetarian mothers who give birth to healthy and happy vegetarian babies.

DIETS FOR CHILDREN

The growing number of vegetarian parents has naturally led to an increase in the number of vegetarian children. Special attention should be given to insure them of the healthiest diet possible for proper physical growth and normal psychological and mental development.

Like adults, children can be well nourished on a well-selected vegetarian diet, even if it contains no animal foods. The trick is to make sure that your child consumes a variety of hearty plant foods, including whole grains and seeds, legumes, fresh fruits and vegetables, and soybean milk fortified with vitamin B-12.

Infants

The best and most natural diet for babies up to one year of age (at least) is mother's milk, which is perfectly balanced for the baby's nutritional needs. Although breast feeding was generally scorned by doctors and nutritionists until the past few years (despite the fact that every baby in the animal kingdom is nourished solely by its mother's milk) most authorities now agree that mother's milk is indeed the best baby food available. In addition to reducing the risk of gastrointestinal problems and possible allergy to cow's milk (which is in fact perfectly formulated for a fast-growing calf) human breast milk provides a satisfying emotional experience for the baby and mother alike. Psychologists say that breast feeding can play a major role in the child's normal emotional development.

Young children

When a vegetarian child is weaned on more solid food, it is important to make sure that his or her diet consists of a variety of foods rich in calcium, iron, riboflavin, vitamin B-12 and zinc—nutrients which are plentiful in well-selected vegetarian diets.

Calcium-rich foods include animal milk, cheese and yogurt. If cow's milk is not used, soymilk fortified with calcium makes a good substitute. Dark green leafy vegetables like spinach, kale, broccoli and turnip greens are good sources of calcium, as are nuts (especially almonds and filberts) which can be made into nut milk or butter. Sunflower seeds, legumes and wholewheat bread are other good sources, and can be prepared for easy eating and digestion.

Since vitamin B-12 is found mostly in animal products, parents of children raised on vegan diets need to be extra careful that the child consumes adequate B-12. In addition to fortified soymilk, some commercial meat analogs and certain brands of brewer's yeast, vitamin B-12 can be taken as a dietary supplement in pill form or is available in sea vegetables, miso and tempeh.

The children's vegeplan

The following Vegeplan is based on the recommendations of Dr. Irma Vyhmeister, Dr. U.D. Register and Ms. L.M. Sonnenberg of the Loma Linda University School of Health.

DAILY VEGEPLAN FOR CHILDREN

Protein Group: Four or more servings, including one serving of milk (animal or fortified soy).

One serving equals   1 cup legumes
2-3 ounces meat analogs
4 tablespoons peanut butter
4 ounces tofu
1½ tablespoons nuts or seeds
1 cup yogurt
1 egg
1 ounce cheese
1 cup milk (animal or soy)

Vegetable Group: Three or more servings, including one serving of a vegetable rich in vitamin C and two servings of leafy green or yellow vegetables.

One serving equals	½ cup cooked vegetables
	1 cup raw vegetables
	½ cup juice

Fruit Group: Three or more servings, including one fruit rich in vitamin C.

One serving equals	½ cup cooked fruit
	1 cup raw fruit
	½ cup juice

Energy-Fiber Group: Four or more servings, including three of whole grains.

One serving equals	1 slice wholewheat bread
	½ to ¾ cup wholegrain cooked cereal
	¾ to 1 cup dry cereal (commercial)
	½-¾ cup wholegrain or enriched noodles
	½ cup granola or muesli cereal
	8 wheat thins
	2 graham crackers
	½ to ¾ cup brown rice

THE CHILD'S DAILY MENU

What would a typical diet plan for vegetarian children be like? While it is somewhat similar to the type of diet enjoyed by adults, the following plan is adopted from recommendations by the nutritionists at the Loma Linda University School of Health and Max Bircher-Benner, M.D., the famous Swiss physician who was a pioneer in preventive medicine through diet.

NINE TO EIGHTEEN MONTHS

BREAKFAST   7-9 ounces of mother's milk OR
                5-5½ ounces of cow's milk with 3½ ounces of oatmeal OR

9 ounces nut milk (diluted nut butter)
1 cup fruit juice

LUNCH Vegetable puree
Mashed potato
Wholewheat cracker or bread
Strained or mashed fruit
Milk (mother's, cow, or fortified soy)

DINNER Oatmeal with grated apple OR
pureed legumes OR
cottage cheese
Wholegrain cracker or bread
Strained cooked fruit

EIGHTEEN MONTHS TO THREE YEARS

BREAKFAST Wholegrain cereal (cooked or fine muesli) OR
1 egg
Milk (animal or fortified soy)
½ sliced bread
Orange juice OR
fresh fruit

LUNCH *Lentil burgers
Potato
Cooked carrots
Tomato and lettuce salad
Wholewheat crackers or bread
Fruit
Milk (animal or fortified soy)

DINNER *Ahimsa pea soup
Peanut butter sandwich on wholewheat bread
Banana
Milk (animal or fortified soy)

THREE TO SIX YEARS

BREAKFAST Orange juice
Wholegrain cereal with fruit OR
1 egg
Wholegrain bread with margarine or sugarless
jelly
Milk (animal or fortified soy)

LUNCH *Lentil burger or TVP meat analog
Potato

Lettuce/sprout/tomato salad
Wholewheat bread or rolls
Fresh fruit
Milk (animal or fortified soy)

DINNER   *Ahimsa pea soup
Peanut butter sandwich on wholegrain bread
Fresh fruit salad with *Freya's topping
Milk (animal or fortified soy)

SIX TO TWELVE YEARS

BREAKFAST   ½ grapefruit
Wholegrain cereal with milk AND/OR
    1 egg
Wholewheat toast with sugarless jelly
Milk (animal or fortified soy)

LUNCH   Lentil burger or TVP meat analog
Potato
Lettuce/sprout/tomato salad with herb dressing
Wholewheat bread or rolls
    *Fruit smoothie (*see* Strawberry smoothie)
Apple

SNACK   2 ounces sunflower seeds with raisins OR
    2 ounces nuts (raw, unsalted) with raisins

DINNER   *Chickpea corn soup
Peanut butter on wholewheat bread
Steamed broccoli
Wholegrain cookies
    *Pineapple-apple drink or milk

sources: I.B. Vyhmeister et al.: "Safe Vegetarian Diets for Children" in *Pediatric Clinics of North America.* February 1977; M. Bircher-Benner. M.D.; *The Children's Diet Book* (New Canaan: Keats Publishing Inc., 1977)

Chapter 7

KEEPING FIT:
DIETS FOR WEIGHT LOSS,
DIETS FOR ATHLETES

Diets for losing weight

There are dozens of diet books and diet plans which tell us how to lose weight. While many plans are little more than diet fads that call for a great deal of sacrifice with uncertain results, other books—like *The Pritikin Program for Diet and Exercise* and *Laurel's Kitchen* —offer sound advice oriented towards weight-reduction without meat.

In spite of the grapefruit diet, the Stillman diet, the all-fiber diet, weight-reducing pills, and dozens of other plans, progressive nutritionists and doctors agree that the best weight-loss plan involves a *change in lifestyle* rather than a rigorous diet to lose weight quickly. Such a change calls for proper eating, daily exercise, adequate rest, and meeting our emotional needs directly so that food is not used as a substitute for a good relationship, physical affection, or as a way to avoid feelings of anger, anxiety or loneliness.

The dietary recommendations made later on in this chapter will help you attain your ideal weight. However, special attention should be given to the following recommendations in order to make the vegetarian weight-loss diet work best for you.

1. Eat mainly wholegrain products, fresh fruits, fresh vegetables and legumes. Since these foods are high in fiber, they will fill you up without providing the empty calories found in so many devitalized, highly processed foods.

2. Reduce your salt and sugar intake. Both are notorious factors in weight gain, and can wreck an otherwise healthy diet. Both are consumed far in excess of our nutritional needs.

3. Avoid alcoholic beverages. They are all high in calories and low in nutrients.

4. Reduce your total amount of fat, especially saturated fat.

5. Engage in pleasurable physical activities every day—walking, dancing, jogging, calisthenics, swimming, yoga.

6. Be aware of your overeating and random snacking and ask yourself if they are substitutes for other needs. Do you need a hug instead of that cupcake? Do you need to yell or pound your fists on the bed instead of eating that dish of ice cream?

7. Substitute high-calorie snack foods with healthy fare—crisp celery or carrot sticks—which are low in calories and high in nutrients and dietary fiber.

The following vegetarian diet plans for weight loss are designed to provide sound nutrition with a minimum of extra calories. They can be used by most people. If you have a chronic overweight problem or have special dietary or medical needs, consult a qualified professional before you experiment with any reducing diet.

THREE-DAY DIET FOR WEIGHT LOSS

DAY 1		**Calories**
BREAKFAST	Cracked wheat cereal (5 ounces cooked) with bran	140
	Raisins (1 tablespoon)	27
	½ cup skimmed animal milk (or (fortified soy milk)	44 (77)
	1 banana	100
	Herb tea	0
	Breakfast	311 (344)
SNACK	1 apple	70
LUNCH	*Hummus (2 tablespoons)	74
	1 piece pita bread	160
	¼ cup alfalfa sprouts	6
	1 medium tomato	27
	Oil & vinegar dressing (2 teaspoons)	54
	Mineral water with lemon	5
	Lunch	384
SNACK	Fresh carrot sticks (1 carrot)	20
	Fresh celery sticks (1 stalk)	5
DINNER	*Vegetarian chili (¾ cup)	171
	Brown rice (½ cup cooked)	116
	Broccoli (1 cup)	40
	1 pat margarine	36
	½ cup grapes	51
	Dinner	414
	TOTAL FOR DAY 1	1206(1239)

DAY 2		
BREAKFAST	1 cup fresh orange juice with 1 tablespoon dried brewer's yeast	112
	1 cup cooked oatmeal	132
	5 medium dates, chopped	108
	1 cup skimmed milk (or fortified soy)	44 (77)
	Breakfast	396 (429)

SNACK	Fresh carrot sticks (1 carrot)	20
LUNCH	*Pasta e fagioli (1 cup)	199
	Tomato and parsley salad (1 tomato with ½ cup fresh parsley)	40
	Oil & vinegar dressing (2 tablespoons)	54
	Peppermint tea	0
	Lunch	293

SNACK	1 cup diced raw pineapple	81
DINNER	*Ahimsa pea soup (1 cup)	251
	Baked potato (1) with chives	100
	Cucumber wedges (¼ cucumber)	15
	½ grapefruit	50
	Dinner	416
	Total for Day 2	1206(1239)

DAY 3

BREAKFAST	1 cup fresh strawberries	55
	1 wholewheat English muffin	120
	1 tablespoon peanut butter	93
	1 cup skimmed milk (or fortified soy)	44 (77)
	Breakfast	312 (345)

SNACK	½ cup raw cauliflower flowers	14
	Fresh celery sticks (from 1 stalk)	7
LUNCH	*Lentil burgers (2 small)	220
	1 slice wholewheat bread	88
	Corn-on-the-cob (1 ear)	70
	1 pat margarine	36
	1 sweet green pepper	15
	1 fresh medium tomato	40
	1 cup canned unsweetened applesauce	100
	Rose hips tea	0
	Lunch	506

SNACK	2 medium peaches	70
DINNER	Ratatouille	195

Alfalfa sprout & cucumber salad (½ cup sprouts and ½ cucumber)	27
Oil & vinegar dressing (2 tablespoons)	54
1 slice wholewheat bread	88
½ banana	50
Grape soda (¼ cup grape juice)	42
Dinner	456
Total Day 3	1365(1388)

Some nutritionists suggest that people on weight-loss diets should take vitamin-mineral supplements for an added margin of safety against possible deficiency. Since most of the food we eat—even the most healthful and natural—comes to us over large distances and after certain periods of storage, some nutritional value may be lost. Although nutritional supplements should never take the place of a sound diet, they provide us with nutritional insurance.

DIETS FOR ATHLETES

For many years we were taught that we couldn't excel as athletes without eating a thick steak with every meal. The prevailing belief was "Protein! Protein! More Protein!" and athletes were ordered to consume large quantities of milk, eggs and especially meat in order to win on the track, football field or in the swimming pool.

Today things are different. Like the early Greek athletes whose diets consisted primarily of fruits, vegetables and whole grains, coaches are telling their athletes to cut down on meat and refined sweets and eat more whole grains, legumes, fruits and vegetables. While a vegetarian diet is no guarantee that you will become a star athlete, it will certainly not prevent you from doing your best.

Since different athletes need different diets (a 90-pound gymnast has different nutritional requirements than a

350-pound weightlifter) only general nutritional guide-lines can be given here.

Vegetarian athletes can easily meet their nutritional needs by following either the Vegeplan for vegans or the Vegeplan for lacto-ovo-vegetarians outlined earlier. Nevertheless, there are certain established guidelines one can follow to help maximize athletic performance. The following ten-point plan is adapted from *Nutrition and the Athlete* by Joseph J. Morella and Richard J. Turletti:

1. Never skip breakfast.

2. Eat regularly: five small meals a day are better than three heavy meals a day. Smaller meals facilitate digestion and put less strain on your body.

3. Eliminate all junk foods (like sugary drinks, candy, refined pastry and sugary desserts) which provide lots of calories but little nutrition.

4. Eliminate foods as much as possible before events, because digestion can interfere with your performance.

5. Eat wholegrain breads and cereals.

6. Eat fortified vegetable oil or margarine rather than butter or animal shortening.

7. Eat lots of fresh fruit every day.

8. Eat four helpings of vegetables every day, especially leafy vegetables. Include dark green or yellow vegetables as well.

9. Drink full-fat (or non-fat with oil added) milk fortified with dry milk solids.

10. Drink a considerable amount of juice and water daily.

Protein: Yes, but not too much

Protein is needed to build muscle tissue, which is important for athletic performance. With a well chosen vegetarian diet—even if it contains all plant foods—a vegetarian athlete can meet his or her protein requirements with ease. While excess protein is broken down by the body and burned as energy, it is also stored as fat—a potential problem for athletes. If you need to increase your protein intake, coaches suggest that the following high protein vegetarian snacks can be enjoyed in addition to the foods recommended in the Vegeplans earlier in this book.

- Skim milk, whole milk, soybean milk
- Milk shakes and soymilk fruit smoothies
- Ice cream (buy only the best, with a minimum of additives)
- Hard-boiled eggs (eaten sparingly)
- Cheese (Swiss, cheddar and other hard cheeses)
- Cottage cheese
- Peanut butter sandwiches on wholegrain bread
- Peanut butter and celery (a favorite of football star Joe Ehrmann)
- Vegetarian tacos
- Vegetarian pizza (preferably with wholewheat crust)
- Vegeburgers (made with lentils, TVP—texturized vegetable protein—or tofu)

Less sugar/more carbohydrates

Over the years our carbohydrate intake has shifted more towards sugars than complex starches, which provide more nourishment and dietary fiber. Unlike sugars, starches (which include cereals, potatoes, legumes and pasta products) provide the highest amount of nutrients per calorie and can be stored by the body for long-term energy. Refined sugars may fool the body into feeling less hunger, but they contribute very little to good nutrition and may actually injure your athletic performance. According to Robert Buxbaum, M.D. and Lyle J. Micheli, M.D. in their book *Sports for Life*, "candy and other sources of sugar are not only unhelpful but have been shown to severely impair performance when eaten just before you exercise."

In addition to their energy value—without the sugar found in sweets or the fat found in meat—carbohydrates from whole food sources provide large amounts of dietary fiber which improves elimination and keeps the body free from toxins. With a meat-oriented diet, these toxins are more likely to remain in your body and cut down on your body's ability to perform at the highest level possible.

Hearty vegetarian snacks provide an abundance of nutritious carbohydrates and are highly favored by successful vegetarian athletes. Between meals, choose from the following list to increase your carbohydrate intake.

- Fruits (fresh and dried)
- Fruit juices (without added sugar)
- Wholegrain breads and pastry (with a minimum of sugar)
- Fruit bars
- Raw, unsalted seeds
- Soy nuts (toasted, unsalted)

Carbohydrate loading

Carbohydrate loading involves a special technique of eating 75-90 percent of carbohydrates for several days before a big race or other athletic event. It is designed to increase the carbohydrate/glycogen stores in the body to help an athlete perform well for an extended period of time. This technique is recommended only for ath-

letes who need to perform for thirty to sixty minutes
and more (such as for a marathon race or long-distance
swim); other athletes tend not to benefit from it. Consult a nutritionist or coach before you decide to experiment with carbohydrate loading.

Before the big event

If you've been eating well in general, chances are
good that you'll be able to perform well on the day of
competition. Experts suggest that athletes should eliminate foods that are high in bulk—like most raw fruits
and vegetables, seeds, wholegrain products and nuts—
just before the event.

The following sample menu plan is adapted from nutritionist Ann Lincoln's recommendations in her book
Food for Athletes:

7:30 AM: *BREAKFAST*	Fresh orange or apple juice Cereal with milk (animal or soy) Egg and enriched toast OR *scrambled tofu on enriched toast Milk (animal or soy)
10:00 AM: *SNACK*	Granola or muesli cereal, dry
12:00 PM: *LUNCH*	*Hearty vegetarian vegetable soup Tofu-sprout sandwich OR cheese sandwich with sprouts Baked potato with chives or sour cream Lettuce wedge with dressing Milk (animal or soy) Baked apple with raisins
4:00 PM: *DINNER*	Artichoke or enriched wheat spaghetti with tomato sauce Baked squash or eggplant Tossed salad Fruit pie Milk (animal or soy)
6:30 PM *(before the 8:00 PM event)* 	Water or fruit juice

Vegetarian athletes enjoy a larger carbohydrate reserve than most meat-eating athletes, and during competition their carbohydrate reserve is burned as long-term energy. When additional energy is required, carbohydrates which are stored in the liver as glycogen are released by the liver and converted to glucose. Vegetarians find that this extra margin of carbohydrate reserve can make the difference between winning and losing an athletic event.

SECTION III

Getting the Most From Your Vegetarian Diet

Chapter 8

FOOD ADDITIVES AND THE VEGETARIAN

BY the end of 1980, it was estimated that we Americans consumed over 800 million pounds of food additives during the previous twelve months—an average of 4½ pounds per person. This was more than a 40 percent increase since 1973. Today more than three thousand chemicals are deliberately added to our food supply, one third of which have never been tested by the government.

Few terms in the English language have caused as much an uproar as "food additives." While most people aren't the least bit concerned about chemicals added to their food, others are extremely worried because many food additives—like MSG, sodium nitrite and saccharin—are dangerous for the body and may lead to degenerative disease like atherosclerosis and cancer.

Let's start by defining our terms. According to the Food and Nutrition Board of the National Research Council, a food additive is "a substance or mixture of substances other than a basic foodstuff which is present in a food as a result of any aspect of production, processing, storage, or packaging."

Food additives fall into several categories with each performing a special role. *Emulsifiers* promote the consistency of foods. *Antioxidants* prevent browning and rancidity. *Food colorings* help a processed food retain a pleasing appearance. *Firming and anticaking agents* retain the texture and consistency of flour used in baking. *Flavorings* are used to restore the food's natural taste lost during processing. *Enrichments* are vitamins and minerals added to foods in an attempt to make up for nutrients lost during the refining process.

Generally speaking, there are four kinds of additives: natural and synthetic, healthy and unhealthy. Natural additives—like lecithin and agar-agar—are derived from plant sources and are considered safe to eat. Sugar and salt are other "natural additives," but can hardly be considered healthy, especially when eaten in the large amounts they are today.

Thousands of other food additives are made in a laboratory from basic chemical elements. While some of these synthetic additives have been found to be relatively safe (like synthetic ascorbic acid) many others (like sodium nitrite) may be dangerous to health. Hundreds of others have not even been tested by the government, and those which have involved experiments on laboratory animals like rabbits, monkeys and mice.

Safety through testing?

While many scientists believe that animal testing is an adequate means of determining the safety of a food additive, critics point out that aside from its inherent cruelty to the animals, vivisection is unreliable because other animal species often react differently than humans do to certain chemicals. According to Dr. J.M. Barnes writing in *World Health Organization Monograph no. 16*, "It must never be forgotten that the results of animal testing may be of little value in forecasting the effects of a substance on man . . ." And Dr.

James D. Gallagher, Director of Research at Lederle Laboratories, said in the *Journal of the American Medical Association*: "Animal studies are done for legal reasons and not for scientific reasons. The predictive value of such studies for man is often meaningless—which means our research may be meaningless."

In addition, laboratory tests often do not evaluate the *synergistic* reactions which may occur when two or more food additives are consumed at the same time. For example, a hot dog cured with sodium nitrate may be generally regarded as safe (GRAS) by itself, but when eaten with buns (preserved with calcium propionate), potato chips (preserved with BHT), beer (preserved with heptyl parabin) and cake (colored with Yellow #6) it is difficult to determine what the overall chemical reaction of these additives may be when eaten together.

The spectre of food additives is a source of deep concern for millions of Americans, who feel that our food supply is becoming completely adulterated with questionable food additives. While the French government permits only seventeen synthetic food flavorings, the United States Food and Drug Administration allows sixteen hundred. Vegetarians are especially concerned about food additives, because the desire for a pure and healthy natural diet is often a major reason for becoming a vegetarian in the first place. While vegetarians naturally avoid all of the hormones, antibiotics and other substances involved in the production of food animals, they are nonetheless concerned about animal by-products (such as gelatin and stearic acid) which are often added to "vegetarian" foods like cake and puddings.

In the following pages we will examine some of the more common food additives and explore their use, origin and overall safety to humans. In addition, we will identify which additives are of animal origin, and suggest alternatives to vegetarians who want to avoid slaughterhouse by-products.

ANTIOXIDANTS

Antioxidants retard the oxidation of unsaturated fats, and prevent foods from losing their flavor and color. They also minimize the destruction of vitamins and keep foods from turning rancid. Antioxidants are added to a wide variety of foods, including baked goods, potato chips, vegetable fats, peanut butter, breakfast cereals, butter and other dairy products, salad oils and dressings, whipped toppings, and imitation fruit drinks.

Alpha Tocopherol (or vitamin E) is a natural antioxidant which prevents oils from going rancid. Vitamin E is found naturally in whole grains, rice germ, dried legumes and vegetable oils. It is safe and nutritious.

Ascorbic Acid (or vitamin C) is a common and safe antioxidant, and is used in soft drinks, cured meats and oily foods. It can be derived from natural sources (including acerola berries, citrus fruits, green peppers and rose hips) or can be synthesized in a laboratory.

BHA (butylated hydroxyanisole) and *BHT* (butylated hydroxytoluene) are the most commonly used synthetic antioxidants and are added (alone and together) to dried breakfast cereals, chewing gum, potato chips, vegetable oil, candy, baked goods, meats, soup mixes and many popular "instant" foods. Although BHA is "generally regarded as safe" (GRAS) by the government, critics claim that it has not been adequately tested. BHT has been found to cause a variety of allergic reactions, including increase of cholesterol levels, and kidney and liver damage. BHT has been banned in Australia, Romania and Sweden.

Propyl Gallate is another synthetic chemical, which is often used with BHA and BHT. It may be added to vegetable oils, processed meat (like bologna and sausage), chicken soup base and potato sticks. The Center for Science in the Public Interest (CSPI) feels that it has not been adequately tested and should be avoided.

EMULSIFIERS

Emulsifiers permit the mixing of two nonmiscible liquids, such as water and oil. Of tremendous popularity in the food industry, over 150 million pounds of emulsifiers are used each year in food production. Natural emulsifiers—like lecithin—were formerly very popular in the food industry and are still used in certain foods like margarine. However most emulsifiers are synthetic, and many are considered of dubious safety. Emulsifiers are used to prolong the shelf life of cake mixes, and insure a uniform texture of dough, ice cream, and candy. They are also used in non-dairy creamers and for dispersing flavor in sherbet and soft drinks.

Bromated Vegetable Oil (BVO) is used mainly in soft drinks and gives a cloudy appearance to citrus flavored beverages. Because BVO remains in body tissues for a long time, the CSPI recommends that it be banned.

Lecithin is a natural emulsifier derived from eggs and soybeans. Used in margarine, baked goods, ice cream and chocolate, it is an important source of the nutrient choline and is reputed to lower serum cholesterol levels.

Mono- and Diglycerides are found mainly in baked goods, margarine, candy and peanut butter. Although added to many "junk" foods like cupcakes and other sweets, they are considered safe by themselves. Since mono- and diglycerides are derived from animal fats, they are often avoided by vegetarians.

Polysorbate 60, 65, and 80 are three related synthetic emulsifiers used extensively in baked goods, prepared desserts and imitation dairy products. They are generally regarded as safe by the U.S. government.

Sodium Carboxymethylcellulose (CMC) is commonly known as cellulose gum. Derived from plants, CMC is used as a stabilizer and thickening agent in addition to an emulsifier. Though primarily added to ice cream to give it a creamier texture, cellulose gum is used in pie fillings, beer, icing, diet foods and candy. CMC is on the GRAS list. However, it has been found to produce arterial lesions in rats, and Dr. Wilhelm C. Heuper, former chief of environmental cancer research at the National Cancer Institute, believes that safer alternatives should be used.

Sodium Monostearate is used primarily in cakes, candy, frozen puddings and prepared icing to keep oil and water from separating. While "generally regarded as safe," this emulsifier is derived from animal products and is therefore avoided by strict vegetarians.

Other common emulsifiers, stabilizers and thickeners include agar-agar and alginates, which are all forms of seaweed. They are safe to eat and contain a variety of important nutrients.

ENRICHMENTS

"Enrichments" include a wide variety of synthetic vitamins and minerals which are added to many processed foods to replace nutrients lost in processing. While touted as superior to more natural foods by cereal and bread manufacturers, enriched food products are basically altered, incomplete and devitalized products which have been "restored" with synthetic (and expensive) nutrients. While the addition of these nutrients is preferable to leaving them out (which would render the foods almost useless nutritionally) they do not provide all of the micronutrients which were refined out during processing. In addition, enrichment may provide too much or too little of the element that was originally in the food.

Because many vegetarians believe that whole, natural, and unrefined foods contain adequate nourishment, they avoid devitalized foods that are artificially enriched. Other people who are concerned about getting enough vitamins and minerals take them in the form of natural multivitamin and mineral supplements. They are far less expensive than getting such nutrients from a cereal box.

FOOD COLORINGS

Food colorings are known in the food industry as "U.S. Certified Colors" and are among the most controversial food additives today. Some food colorings occur naturally in nature, and include annato, carotene and chlorophyll. They are generally regarded as safe, and have been used for hundreds—if not thousands—of years. However, the history of synthetic food dyes (most of which are coal tar derivatives) is tainted by scandal.

While some synthetic dyes are less dangerous than others, most are used extensively in foods with little or no nutritional value, like soda pop, candy and gelatin desserts. Over the years most of the coal tar colorings have been banned by the Food and Drug Administration, because they were linked to cancer and other diseases. The following food colorings are permitted "provisionally" pending results of animal tests. At the present time, over 4 million pounds of coal tar dyes are added each year to food, cosmetics and textiles.

Red No. 3 (Erythrosine) is used in processed cherries, candy and baked goods. It is a suspected carcinogen.

Red No. 40 (Allura) is used in soda pop, pastry, gelatin desserts, sausage and pet food. It was found to induce bladder cancer in rats and mice.

Citrus Red No. 2 is another artificial coloring used to color the skins of certain Florida oranges, and is consumed when we peel the orange with our teeth or eat marmalade or candied rind. It is a suspected carcinogen and has produced serious bladder abnormalities in rats.

Yellow No. 5 (Tartrazine) is used in gelatin desserts, candy, pet food, and pastry. Critics say that it has not been adequately tested and that many people are allergic to it.

Yellow No. 6 (Sunset Yellow FCF) is regarded as a safer

alternative to tartrazine, although it also produces allergic reactions in humans. It is used in the making of sausage as well as numerous junk foods like candy, gelatin and fruity drinks.

Green No. 3 (Forest Green FCF) is mostly added to candy and soft drinks. The CSPI suggests that it needs more extensive testing and therefore should be avoided.

Blue No. 1 (Brilliant Blue FCF) is used in soft drinks, candy and baked goods. Found to produce tumors in laboratory animals, it is banned in the British Commonwealth.

Blue No. 2 (Ingotine) is added to beverages, candy and pet food. Short term studies showed that it produces blood changes and liver abscesses in pigs.

FLAVORINGS AND SWEETENERS

According to the noted food expert Beatrice Trum Hunter, more than $150 million worth of flavoring additives are used annually in foods and beverages in the United States. While many natural flavorings like salt, pepper and cloves have been used for thousands of years, the astronomical increase in consumption of convenience foods has fostered the use of hundreds of synthetic and refined flavorings which are often added to food without our knowledge. Many of these additives are derived from natural sources and include sugar, salt and even monosodium glutamate, which are not necessarily good for us. Since most flavorings are added to highly processed foods, they are meant to replace the natural food flavors which were refined out. For this reason, nutritionists suggest that we eat the food in its natural state (with its natural flavor) to which we can add our own flavoring according to individual taste. Since many processed foods contain far more flavoring than we would use ourselves, we increase our chances of consuming potentially harmful additives that are designed to salvage a food from tastelessness.

Artificial Flavorings are used by the hundreds in the food industry, and are rarely listed by name. While many flavoring chemicals also occur in nature and are probably safe, many (up to 600) are combined with others to form a flavoring compound and are therefore difficult to test. Artificial flavorings are used extensively in soda pop, candy, breakfast cereals, gelatin desserts, baked goods, syrups, chewing gum and seasonings. They have been found to cause abnormal changes in laboratory animals, and are held to be a factor in hyperactivity among children.

Corn Syrup is used mostly to sweeten and thicken low-nutrition foods like candy, syrups and snack foods. A thick liquid manufactured from cornstarch, it promotes tooth decay and—aside from calories—has no nutritional value.

Fructose (see Table Sugar)

Glucose (see Table Sugar)

Hydrolyzed Vegetable Protein (HVP) is a flavor enhancer derived primarily from soybeans. When protein is hydrolyzed the individual amino acids are released in free form, and like MSG, adds flavor to processed foods. Added primarily to instant soups, processed meats, beef stew and sauce mixes, it has been found to cause brain damage in baby mice.

Monosodium Glutamate (MSG) is added to over ten thousand different processed food items in America each year to the tune of 40 million pounds. Long popular in Chinese restaurants to "hold" the flavor of foods, MSG is used in almost every processed food available: canned foods, meat tenderizers, frozen foods, TV dinners, condiments and seasonings, salad dressing, baked goods, processed meats, seafood, and a host of other products including animal feed.

MSG is popular because it restores taste to foods whose taste has been lost due to processing. Without it, many refined foods would have little or no taste at all.

Monosodium glutamate also helps retard the oxidation of foods and gives them a longer shelf life.

Although derived from natural sources (sugar beets, seaweed, soybeans, wheat gluten and corn gluten), MSG is highly refined and has been found to destroy brain cells of laboratory animals. It also has caused tightness in the chest, headache and a burning sensation in the neck of human beings. Public pressure led some food processors to stop using MSG in baby foods.

Saccharin is a synthetic sweetener used extensively in "diet" candy, soft drinks, baked goods and canned fruit. In 1977, the Food and Drug Administration proposed that saccharin be banned because it produced cancer in laboratory animals, and a National Academy of Sciences panel concluded that saccharin also posed a potential cancer risk to humans. Because an estimated one-third of children under ten years of age consume products that contain saccharin (especially soft drinks) the long-term cancer risks of this age group are of special concern to parents, medical doctors and health educators.

Salt (Sodium Chloride) is used extensively (and liberally) in nearly every processed food, especially soups, potato chips, crackers and canned vegetables. Used by humans for nearly three thousand years as a condiment and food preservative, salt provides sodium, an important nutrient. However, excessive sodium can raise blood pressure and is a factor in heart attack and stroke. Nutritionists suggest that a diet of fresh, natural foods contains adequate sodium and that other seasonings— such as kelp powder, "vegit" or gomasio—can be used instead.

Sorbitol is a sugar alcohol which is used to sweeten and thicken foods; it also helps retain moisture content. Because it contains slightly fewer calories than ordinary table sugar, it is used mostly in dietetic foods and drinks, candy, shredded coconut and ice cream. Although on the "GRAS" list, sorbitol (as well as the similar chemical mannitol) has been known to cause diarrhea in both children and adults.

Sucrose (table sugar) is a highly refined product derived from sugar cane and sugar beets. Because sweetened and sugared foods appeal to most people, refined sugar makes up one-sixth of our average diet and we consume about 120 (some say 200) pounds of it a year.

Most of the refined sugar we consume is hidden in processed foods. Meat products contain nearly three percent added sugar by weight, while 13 percent of processed vegetables is added sugar. "Natural" granola cereals can contain up to 23 percent sucrose, while many popular breakfast cereals contain between 40 and 68 percent added sugar. Sucrose contains no nutrients other than calories, and is a factor in tooth decay, diabetes, obesity, hypoglycemia, and increased levels of tryglycerides (or free fatty acids). In addition, sugar requires certain vitamins (like thiamin) to metabolize it. The more sugar we consume, the likelier it is that vitamin deficiencies can occur.

Brown Sugar is prepared by pouring a small amount of molasses over pure granulated sugar. Though often touted as a "health food," brown sugar is only slightly less harmful to you than white sugar. *Turbinado sugar* (or raw sugar) is also essentially the same as white sugar and contains more than 99 percent sucrose.

Fructose and *Glucose* (also known as Dextrose) are natural sugars which are also added to many foods. While they both contain sweetening properties, they are absorbed more slowly by the body than sucrose and are thought to be less likely to trigger hypoglycemic attacks. *Honey* contains an abundance of these sugars in addition to trace minerals. It is often preferred to table sugar. While fructose, glucose and dextrose are less unhealthy than table sugar, they should be consumed in moderation. They occur naturally in fresh fruit and their juice.

Because table sugar is sometimes filtered through animal bones during processing, strict vegetarians refuse to eat it. Vegans often reject honey because they feel that it involves the exploitation (and sometimes the death) of bees.

PRESERVATIVES

Preservatives are substances added to foods to keep them from spoiling or going rancid. Some specifically delay food spoilage caused by molds, ropes, yeasts and bacteria, while others prevent chemical changes which affect color, flavor, texture or appearance.

Calcium (or Sodium) Propionate is a chemical preservative used primarily as a mold- and rope-inhibitor in bread, rolls and other baked goods, and can give stale foods the appearance of freshness. While propionic acid occurs naturally in cheese manufacture, the chemicals used by bakers are made synthetically from ethylene, carbon monoxide and steam. Though it is generally regarded as safe, gastrointestinal disturbances and headaches have been linked to propionates.

Sodium Nitrate and Sodium Nitrite are synthetic preservatives used in processed meats like ham, bacon, hot dogs and bologna. Nitrate and nitrite prevent botulism bacteria from forming, and give processed meat a fresh, red color.

Human toxicity to these substances is well established. Nitrite can lead to the formation of potent cancer-causing chemicals known as nitrosamines. While not as toxic as sodium nitrite, sodium nitrate slowly breaks down into nitrite. Since these chemicals are both used extensively in processed meat and cured fish, vegetarians, by virtue of their diet, conveniently avoid them altogether.

Sodium Benzoate is used to control the growth of microorganisms in acidic foods like fruit juice, carbonated drinks, pickles, jams and jellies. It is generally considered safe.

Sodium Bisulfite (a powder) and *Sulfur Dioxide* (a gas) have been used to protect color changes in dried fruits and to prevent bacterial growth in wine, soups, juices and other foods. They both destroy vitamin B-1 and have been linked to gastric disturbances, headache and diarrhea in humans.

Many other elements are routinely added to food. EDTA, for example, is a chelating agent which traps metal impurities which get into food during processing. It is used in soft drinks, canned foods, beer and salad dressings. We may consume up to a hundred milligrams or more EDTA daily. The extensive use of chelating agents like EDTA (over forty others are approved by the Food and Drug Administration) may make it difficult for us to absorb adequate trace minerals in our diets which can lead to mineral deficiency.

Gelatin is a thickening and jelling agent used in gelatin desserts, yogurt, cheese spreads and ice cream. Because it is made from the bones and hooves of slaughtered animals, it is avoided by vegetarians. They instead use agar, a gelatin-like extract from a seaweed.

Glycerine, which maintains water content in foods, is regarded as a safe additive to marshmallows, baked goods, and candy. Since it is usually obtained from slaughtered animals, it is avoided by many vegetarians.

Additives: what to do

What are we to do about all these food additives? While it is difficult (if not impossible) to avoid them completely, there are several ways to sharply eliminate them from our diets.

In the first place, read the food labels. While many additives (water, spices or agar agar) may not be harmful, others may not be good for you. Compare product labels to see which foods are free of harmful additives.

Additives are used primarily in highly processed and convenience foods. By simply choosing foods which are as close as possible to their natural state, we can eliminate the majority of food additives. Since many additives are used in meat processing, becoming a vegetarian means that you will avoid the preservatives, nitrites, nitrates, artificial colorings, pesticides and drug residues involved in the raising, slaughtering, preparation and packaging of livestock.

One of the purposes of this book is to show how you can enjoy a wide variety of easy-to-prepare healthy foods which do not contain harmful (or possibly-harmful) food additives. By carefully reading the chapters on "How to Survive in a Health Food Store—In Style," "Menu Plans for Vegetarians" and "Recipes for Life" you will be able to enjoy a healthy and varied diet which contains no chemical "surprises" in the form of food additives.

Chapter 9

MEDICINAL FOODS: HEALING FROM THE GARDEN

WHILE most of our food is noted for its nutritional value, we often overlook the subtle medicinal properties of many vegetables, fruits, grains and herbs. Used by many Americans since colonial times, medicinal plants are now being examined by modern scientists to determine their true medicinal value. In his book *Diet & Nutrition*, Rudolph Ballentine, M.D., cites that cranberry juice was a popular folk remedy among New Englanders, who drank it to relieve urinary infections. Modern researchers found that certain chemicals found naturally in cranberry juice convert to hippuric acid, which, when combined with other substances, appears to kill bacteria in the urinary tract.

In addition to their nutritional value, foods from the vegetarian cornucopia can gently soothe your nerves after a long day at the office, they can help you warm up on a cold day, help purify your system, and get you to sleep if you are tense. While not actually medicines, many vegetarian foods contain tiny amounts of natural medicinal elements which can improve your health and help you enjoy a more productive life. On the following pages we will examine some of the more common medicinal foods and see how they can be used to maximum benefit. However, please remember that this is not a "do-it-yourself" course in natural medicine to be used instead of the services of a professional. Aside from delaying proper treatment of disease, if eaten in excess some of these ordinarily healthy foods (especially the herbs and spices) can have adverse effects.

Medicinal foods can be easily enjoyed as part of a healthful vegetarian diet. You probably use most of them already in soups, salads, casseroles and tea. In the recommended reading section of this book, we'll include several "how-to" books on medicinal herbs and plants which will provide you with more specific and complete information.

Nature's medicine chest

Analgesics are substances which have the ability to relieve or diminish pain.

Anthelmintics are able to destroy and expel intestinal worms.

Aperients are mild stimulants for the bowels and help them eliminate toxins better.

Aromatics have an agreeable odor and are known for their stimulating qualities.

Astringents contract organic tissues, thus reducing the flow of secretions and other discharges.

Calmatics, true to their name, have a mild tranquilizing and sedative effect on the body.

Cathartics are known for their laxative effects.

Demulcents are substances which soothe irritated tissues, especially mucous membranes.

Depuritives cleanse and purify the system (and especially the blood) of toxic materials.

Diuretics are agents which, when taken internally, increase the flow of urine.

Emollients are used to soothe irritation and to soften tissues.

Expectorants promote the discharge of mucus from the respiratory passages.

Laxatives help produce a normal bowel movement.

Restoratives restore consciousness or normal physiological activity.

Stimulants have the ability to excite or quicken activity of the body's physiological processes.

Tonics strengthen or invigorate the body or its organs.

FRUITS AND NUTS

Many common fresh fruits have outstanding medicinal properties, and have been used as folk remedies in this country (and abroad) for hundreds of years. While most fruits can be eaten directly or in the form of fruit salads, their medicinal properties are concentrated when taken in the form of fresh juices. Nuts are made into poultices or enjoyed as nut butter or milk.

Almond

Almond kernels (unsalted) are of most value when eaten raw. They soothe irritated mucous membranes, and can be made into a poultice to soothe irritated skin.

Apple

The fruit of the apple—when eaten whole—is said to be a mild, non-irritating laxative, while peeled or ground apples are good for diarrhea. Herbalists claim that apples are good for people who suffer from diabetes and hyperacidity and help purify the liver and kidneys. Apple peels can be used as a tea, and are said to help those suffering from rheumatic illness.

Black Walnut

Raw, unsalted black walnut meats are believed to help people suffering from tuberculosis, ringworm, skin rash and intestinal parasites.

Cherry

Fresh cherries are known for their refreshing, cleansing effect on body tissues.

Currants
Black currants are said to be good for kidney problems, while red currants are used to promote the appetite and help relieve upset stomachs.

Fig
Figs are known for their mild laxative properties, and are often taken to help expel intestinal worms.

Grape
Fresh grapes or grape juice are said to calm the nerves, dissolve calcium deposits, stimulate acid secretion in the stomach and cleanse the blood. Grapes are known as excellent body cleansers and purifiers and are often used when fasting. Grape pits contain small amounts of Laetrile and are often chewed along with the fruit as a cancer preventative.

Lemon
The fruit or juice of fresh lemons is known for its depuritive and anti-arthritic properties, and is used by people suffering from intestinal infections, colds and coughs. When applied externally, lemon juice is an effective astringent and skin softener.

Melon
Fresh melons of all types are known for their refreshing and cleansing properties. They also aid digestion.

Olive
Olive oil is an effective laxative, and is said to reduce serum cholesterol levels in the body. It is also used to expel intestinal worms. When used externally, olive oil (which is high in vitamin E) is used for burns, insect bites and general itching.

Orange
The fruit and juice of the orange are depuritives, disinfectants, mineralizers and light stimulants.

Papaya
The fruit of the papaya aids digestion and is used in Latin America for the treatment of allergies.

Peach
Fresh peaches are said to aid digestion.

Pear
Pears are known for easy digestion and are generally good for the intestines.

Plum
In addition to their excellent laxative properties, plums also promote appetite and aid digestion.

Pomegranate
The seeds of this delicious fruit are eaten to help expel intestinal worms and are known for their astringent qualities.

Pumpkin
Pumpkin seeds are known for their ability to expel tapeworm.

Raspberry
Fresh raspberries are known for their mild laxative properties when eaten in large quantities.

Tomato
Tomatoes are popular for their ability to stimulate the liver and help purify the body of toxins.

VEGETABLES AND GRAINS

Alfalfa
Alfalfa sprouts improve the appetite, and are believed to relieve urinary and bowel problems.

Artichoke
The flowering head of the artichoke is an effective diuretic and sedative. In addition, the artichoke has won a reputation as an aphrodisiac.

Asparagus
The fresh young shoots of this vegetable are known for their diuretic, aperient and sedative qualities. They are used to increase cellular activity in the kidneys, and

to encourage the evacuation of the bowels. Asparagus is also recommended by herbalists for gouty and rheumatic problems.

Barley

Known primarily for its demulcent properties, cooked barley with milk is good for stomach and intestinal irritation, and is often used to relieve fever. When applied externally, barley is good for skin infections.

Bean

Generally speaking, beans—including kidney, green, navy, pinto, snap, string and wax beans—are good diuretics and are said to lower blood sugar levels.

Beet

In addition to being rich in minerals, beets are used medicinally for their laxative and diuretic effects.

Cabbage

Fresh cabbage (both green and purple) is considered useful towards relieving respiratory infections, dysentery and anemia.

Carrot

In addition to preventing night blindness, carrots are anthelmintics (eliminating intestinal worms), diuretics and stimulants. They are natural purifiers and help cleanse the intestine. Fresh carrot juice is held to relieve stomach acidity and heartburn while carrot soup is said to help relieve diarrhea.

Celery

Fresh celery sticks and leaves are extremely medicinal and are popular for their tonic effects. Celery promotes perspiration, calms the nerves and helps stimulate the appetite. Celery juice is considered good for rheumatism and gout, flatulence and liver problems in general.

Chives

Freshly picked chives help stimulate the appetite and promote digestion.

Corn

Corn silk is often used as a tea to relieve kidney and bladder problems.

Cucumber

Cucumber is a popular aperient and diuretic. When eaten alone or in a salad, cucumber is believed to dissolve uric acid and help relieve chronic constipation. Fresh cucumber juice is good for the intestines, liver, kidneys and skin. When used externally, cucumber juice makes a soothing and effective eyewash.

Dandelion

Dandelion leaves are rich in iron and other minerals. When used in a salad or as an ingredient in vegetable juice, the leaves are said to purify the blood and help relieve kidney and liver problems.

Garlic

Long considered a powerful medicinal plant by people the world over, garlic stimulates the activity of the digestive organs and regulates the action of the liver and gall bladder. It is said to relieve intestinal infections as well as problems due to putrefactive intestinal bacteria. Garlic is also believed to help expel intestinal worms, especially when garlic juice and water are used together in an enema.

Horseradish

Horseradish root is a good diuretic, and is used to relieve gout, rheumatism and bladder infections.

Jerusalem Artichoke

The Jerusalem artichoke is said to be good for people with diabetes and other pancreas-related ailments.

Kelp

Sea kelp is a potent mineralizer, and is good for the thyroid, pituitary and adrenal glands.

Leek

Leeks have medicinal values similar to but milder

than garlic. They stimulate the appetite, help relieve congestion of the respiratory passages and are an effective non-irritating diuretic.

Lettuce

Lettuce leaves (all types) are excellent purifiers, expectorants and sedatives. They are considered to be effective calming agents for people with insomnia and nervous conditions.

Oat

In addition to its nutrient properties, cooked oatmeal is good for people with liver problems and helps relieve dyspepsia and gastroenteritis.

Onion

Onions are highly regarded for their ability to purify the blood and for their sedative and diuretic properties. When taken internally, fresh onion juice is said to lower blood pressure and strengthen the heart. When applied to the skin, onion juice is good for disinfecting wounds and relieving skin eruptions.

Pepper

In addition to their high vitamin and mineral content, peppers are said to aid digestion.

Potato

Boiled or baked potatoes help relieve stomach aches and are known for their anti-arthritic properties.

Radish

Radishes are known for their cleansing properties, and are believed to help relieve diarrhea, flatulence, insomnia and bronchial inflammation.

Rhubarb

Cooked rhubarb stems are eaten for their astringent and laxative qualities, and are believed to relieve intestinal infections. The leaves of the rhubarb plant are poisonous.

Spinach

Fresh spinach is a little known blood purifier and laxative.

Watercress

Fresh watercress is a good blood purifier, and is extremely high in minerals. It has been used to stimulate glandular activity and to relieve mild digestive disturbances.

HERBS AND SPICES

Basil

A popular herb used in cooking, basil is an appetizer and antispasmotic. When used as a tea, it is said to relieve stomach cramps, vomiting and coughs.

Chamomile

Chamomile flowers, when used as a tea, are a popular aromatic and antispasmotic. Chamomile tea is also good for relieving headaches and promoting sleep.

Caraway

Ground caraway seeds are a popular garnish for vegetable soup and potatoes. They help increase appetite and digestion. Caraway is also known for its mild expectorant qualities.

Cayenne

A powerful stimulant, small amounts of cayenne are said to be good for the spleen, kidney and pancreas.

Cloves

The flower buds of cloves are a reputed aphrodisiac.

Dill

Dill is a popular seasoning, and is used medicinally as an aromatic and stimulant. Known as a useful stomach remedy for hundreds of years, it prevents gas and fermentation. Dill is also believed to quiet the nerves.

Ginger

Fresh ginger is a recognized stimulant and expectorant, and helps ease the effect of colds and digestive cramps. Ginger tea is considered an effective cleanser for the entire body.

Golden Seal

When used as a tea, golden seal root activates the mucous membranes and helps relieve catarrhal conditions. It increases the appetite, aids digestion, and relieves bladder problems. Some people use golden seal tea as a mouthwash, vaginal douche, and as an excellent wash to relieve skin diseases.

Marjoram

This popular herb is a well-known tonic, expectorant and calmative. When used as a tea, marjoram is good for upset stomach, indigestion, coughs and nervousness.

Mint

Mint—both peppermint and spearmint—is often enjoyed as a tea to relieve nervousness, insomnia, cramps, headache and nausea. Mint leaves make a popular additive to bath water to help relieve itchy skin. When eaten in quantity, fresh mint leaves are considered an aphrodisiac.

Mustard

A popular garnish for vegetables and sauces, small amounts of mustard seed are used to stimulate appetite and blood circulation. Large amounts are said to be irritating.

Parsley

In addition to being rich in minerals, fresh parsley is believed to have strong aperient and diuretic properties. It is taken to relieve congestion in the kidneys, liver and spleen. Jethro Kloss refers to parsley as a "preventive herb for cancer" in his book *Back to Eden*.

Sage

This popular herb is used medicinally in tea to help reduce sweating and relax the nerves.

Savory

As a tea, savory is good for the stomach, and is used to relieve intestinal disorders.

Sorrel

Sorrel is used primarily as a condiment in soups and salads, but is used medicinally as a tea. It is believed to be good for the heart and the liver, and aids in purifying the system in general.

Thyme

Thyme is one of the best known old-time remedies. As a tonic, antiseptic and antispasmodic, it is reputed to strengthen the lungs, ease stomach cramps and relieve headaches.

Chapter 10

SURVIVING IN A HEALTH FOOD STORE—WITH STYLE

WHEN Susan G. first became a vegetarian, she thought she would be able to choose from only a few dozen foods—three or four varieties of beans, several types of cereals, and the vegetables (like carrots, cucumbers and iceberg lettuce) she had eaten since childhood. After reading a few vegetarian cookbooks, however, Susan was pleased to learn that a vegetarian diet goes far beyond the ordinary, and can include an impressive selection of foods with names like tabouli, tahini, couscous and kombu.

Today's health and natural food stores offer an abundance of exciting and exotic foods which can make the vegetarian alternative a lifetime adventure. There are ethnic foods from around the world which have been enjoyed for centuries. And there are new foods native to the United States being used in dozens of appealing ways.

On the following pages we'll explore some of the unfamiliar foods—and see how they can be enjoyed in delicious, nutritious and creative vegetarian meals.

Acidophilus

Acidophilus contains "friendly" bacteria which promote the growth of healthy intestinal flora while inhibiting the growth of dangerous bacteria. Similar to yogurt (only much stronger) it is often taken in liquid form as a nutritional supplement.

Adzuki Beans

Very popular with macrobiotics, adzuki beans are dark red beans imported from Japan. They can be eaten alone or with rice or whole grains.

Agar Agar

Agar Agar is a vegetable gelatin derived from a type of seaweed. Favored by vegetarians over animal gelatin, agar agar will jell salads and desserts and makes an excellent soup thickener.

Artichoke Noodles

Artichoke noodles are made from the Jerusalem artichoke, a tuber-bearing type of sunflower. Highly nutritious and lower in carbohydrates than wheat noodles, artichoke noodles are often sold as "imitation spaghetti" because they contain no wheat flour.

Bancha Tea

A strong, bracing tea popular with macrobiotics, it is made from tea leaves and stems that have been aged on the tree for three years. Bancha tea is excellent when you have a cold because it cleanses and warms the entire body.

Barley

Barley is our oldest cultivated grain and goes back to Biblical times. Whole barley is sold with the bran (and the nutrients the bran provides) while pearled barley is what's left when the hull and bran are removed. Barley is a nutritious and inexpensive food which can be used in place of rice. It is especially good in soups.

Bran

Bran is the high fiber coating of the wheat and rice kernel. Though extremely rich in vitamins and minerals, much of the bran used in this country is fed directly to livestock. People often sprinkle bran on their morning cereal to increase its fiber content.

Brewer's Yeast

Originally a by-product of the brewing industry, brewer's yeast is a veritable treasure of B vitamins and important minerals. Available as a nutritional supplement in powder, flake or pill form, brewer's yeast is added to juice, bread, stews and soups. Remember that this is not baker's yeast, which will rise when added to water.

Buckwheat

Also known as kasha, buckwheat is a nutritious staple in Russia and Eastern Europe which is now gaining popularity in the United States. An extremely hardy grain (which is relatively free from insecticides) buckwheat makes an excellent cereal, stuffing or rice substitute. It can also be used as flour or grits.

Bulgur

Like many other grains, bulgur comes to us from the Middle East. It is wheat that has been steamed, dried and cracked, and has all the nutrients of whole wheat. *Couscous* is a more refined form of bulgur, and is lighter in color and less nutritious. Bulgur is popular in cereals, salads and is a primary ingredient in tabouli (see recipes).

Carob

Also known as St. John's Bread, carob comes from a tree in the form of pods, which are eventually ground into powder. A source of minerals and vitamin A, carob is a popular chocolate substitute.

Chickpeas

Also known as garbanzo beans, chickpeas are excellent in casseroles, soups and salads. Hummus, made from cooked, mashed chickpeas, is a spectacular bean dip from the Middle East. Directions for making hummus can be found in the recipe section of this book.

Daikon

Daikon is a large, white Japanese radish. It can be eaten either chopped or sautéed with rice or other cooked vegetables.

Date Sugar

A mineral-rich substitute for cane sugar and honey, date sugar is made from the sap of the date palm tree.

Dulse

Dulse is a light, deep purple seaweed which is very rich in iodine. You can eat it dry like candy, or enjoy it sprinkled on soup and salad.

Fava Beans

Also known as broad beans, favas are large lima-shaped beans popular in Mediterranean countries. They are good in soups and casseroles, but require extra seasoning to compensate for their bland taste.

Ginseng

A popular medicinal plant used in the Orient for thousands of years, ginseng is considered a rejuvenator of male sexuality, and is claimed to strengthen the stomach, promote appetite, and keep the heart young and healthy. The kind of ginseng you buy at the store comes from the root of the plant and can be found in liquid, capsule, powdered or root form.

Gluten Flour

When the starch is removed from wheat flour, you're left with wheat gluten—an elastic substance high in nutrients. While some people are allergic to gluten, others use gluten flour as a high-protein meat substitute. When mixed with wheat flour and water, gluten can be made into a stiff dough which can be shaped and cut into "steaks," "roasts" and "chops." For that reason, it is a popular base for any commercial textured vegetable protein foods sold in health food stores as meat substitutes.

Gomasio

Despite its exotic name, gomasio is simply a mixture of sea salt and sesame seeds. Long favored as a seasoning by macrobiotics, gomasio does not stimulate thirst as does salt alone.

Graham Flour

Named after Rev. Sylvester Graham (a pioneer American vegetarian), this flour is made from wholegrain winter wheat. It is especially popular in Graham crackers, a familiar snack for millions.

Hijiki

A delicious brown stringlike seaweed from Japan, hijiki is served as a popular appetizer in many Japanese restaurants. Ounce for ounce, hijiki contains thirteen times the calcium of milk.

Kefir

Kefir, like yogurt, is a type of fermented milk. Popular in Eastern Europe, the Middle East and parts of Asia, kefir provides the body with lots of friendly bacteria while it kills harmful strains of bacteria in the intestine.

Kelp

This brown seaweed contains extraordinary amounts of minerals, especially iron, calcium and iodine. It also contains an abundance of vitamin B-12. Kelp is sold in tablet and powdered form as a seasoning and nutritional supplement, but many vegetarians prefer to cut small pieces of kelp and add them to soups, casseroles, salads and stir-fried dishes.

Kombu

Kombu is a type of kelp from Japan.

Kudzo

Kudzo (or kuzu) is a tuberous root from Japan which was introduced to the southern United States to prevent soil erosion. Like powdered arrowroot, kudzo is an excellent (and nutritious) thickener for soups and gravies.

Lecithin

Lecithin is a popular nutritional supplement used to help lower serum cholesterol. Found primarily in egg yolks, soybeans and nonhydrogenated oils, lecithin is available in granules, as a liquid and in capsules. Add it to soup, stews and baked goods, or enjoy it in juice.

Lentils

An ancient legume dating back to Biblical times, lentils—both brown and red—are high in protein, vitamins and minerals. They can be enjoyed in a variety of inexpensive soups, salads, "burgers" and casseroles. Lentil sprouts can be used in stir-fried dishes, but tend to be bitter when eaten raw. See the recipe section for several gourmet lentil dishes.

Milk (Certified Raw)

Unpasteurized milk which has to meet high standards of quality is often "certified raw" by the government. Because it isn't subjected to high temperatures in processing, raw milk is naturally higher in protein, vitamins A and D, potassium, phosphorus and calcium.

Milk (Soy)

Soy milk is sold in liquid and powdered form, and is sometimes fortified with vitamin B-12. It is used primarily for babies who are allergic to animal milk, and by strict vegetarians (vegans) who eschew all animal products. Use soy milk as you would use cow's milk as a refreshing beverage and in shakes, soups, cereals and baking.

Millet

Millet is an ancient seed-like grain long popular in

India, Africa and the Middle East. Enjoy it as a breakfast cereal in place of oatmeal. Add it to flour for baking, use it as a base for casseroles, or try it as a nutritious rice substitute.

Miso

Miso is a fermented soybean paté that has been aged for three years. In addition to soybeans and salt, miso contains other ingredients: rice and soybeans make *kome miso*, barley and soy make *mugi miso*, while soybeans alone are called *hacho miso*. Enjoy miso as a flavoring or soup base. Like yogurt, miso has a beneficial effect on intestinal bacteria and is a source of vitamin B-12 for strict vegetarians. Do not boil miso, because high temperatures destroy its friendly bacteria.

Molasses

When you boil sugar cane juice and extract the raw sugar, you are left with molasses. While high in minerals (especially iron) molasses also tends to be high in pollutants which are left over from sugar processing. Use molasses to flavor cereals, shakes and yogurt.

Muesli

The Swiss answer to granola, muesli was first introduced by Dr. Max Bircher-Benner, a Swiss physician and naturopath, over fifty years ago. Made of raw oats, seeds, wheat germ, chopped nuts, and dried fruits, *Bircher muesli* is a delicious cereal loaded with nutrients. While available ready-mixed, you can prepare your own at one-third the cost. To find out, refer to the recipe section.

Mu Tea

Mu Tea is an exotic, bracing tea made from sixteen different herbs and spices.

Mung Beans

Originally from India, mung beans are small green beans which can be enjoyed in a variety of ways. They are most popular as sprouts, and can be included in salads, sandwiches and stir-fried dishes.

Nori

An exotic Japanese seaweed which is very rich in nutrients, nori is sold dry in thin sheets. While some chefs use nori to roll around other vegetables, most people toast it and serve it crumbled over soups, rice and casseroles.

Oats

This popular grain is available in two basic forms: *Rolled oats* are hulled and flattened on steel rollers, which makes them easier to cook. *Steel cut oats* are not as heavily processed, but they take longer to cook. Oats aren't only for breakfast. Enjoy them in casseroles, oatmeal burgers (see recipe), oat bread and as a thickener for soups and gravies.

Papain

Papain is an enzyme extracted from the papaya fruit. It is taken to aid digestion.

Pignolia Nuts (Pine Nuts)

These delicious soft buttery nuts are high in protein, fat and essential minerals. Add as a garnish to spaghetti sauce, casseroles and vegetables, because they are very expensive.

Pinto Beans

A popular speckled bean that is beige in color, pintos are great in soups, salads and Mexican refried beans (fríjolés refritos).

Pistachio Nuts

Although most people know pistachios by their red shell and salty taste, the best pistachio nuts are of the natural variety: brown in color, lightly roasted and without added salt. Grown in Asia and the Middle East, pistachio nuts are high in protein, vitamins and minerals.

Pumpkin Seeds

Dried pumpkin seeds are good raw or roasted. Enjoy them as a hearty snack or use them to garnish soups, salads, and casseroles. Pumpkin seeds are very high in protein, and contain an abundance of B vitamins and minerals.

Rice (Brown)

Compared with white rice, from which the nutritious germ and bran has been refined, brown rice is higher in protein, fiber and trace nutrients. Organic brown rice contains no insecticides or other poisons, and is available in short-grain or long-grain forms.

Rice (Wild)

Wild rice isn't really rice at all, but the seed of tall aquatic grasses native to North America. Wild rice is very costly. While you can eat it alone as you would "ordinary" rice, most people mix it with brown rice for an exotic side dish.

Rice Bran

Made from the outer husk of the rice grain, rice bran is often sprinkled on cereal and yogurt, or added to baked goods.

Rose Hips

Rose hips are the urn-shaped receptacles at the base of the rose blossom. In addition to a popular tea rich in vitamin C, rose hips form the base for natural vitamin C supplements.

Royal Jelly

Royal jelly is a pale sweet substance made by worker bees for their queen. Since it helps the queen bee live for so long, people take royal jelly to preserve beauty and attain long life.

Rye

This well-known grain is harvested in Northern Europe, Canada and the northern United States. High in protein, B vitamins and potassium, rye is a popular cereal and flour.

Sea Salt

Sea salt is what is left over after sea water is evaporated. While not exactly a "health food," sea salt contains natural iodine and other trace minerals ordinary land salt often lacks.

Sesame Oil

Unlike other vegetable oils, sesame oil has a pungent, exotic taste. Use it in sauces, salad dressings and stir-fried dishes.

Sesame Tahini

A delicious butter made from toasted sesame seeds, tahini makes an excellent sandwich spread. Add it to stir-fried dishes, casseroles, salad dressings and sauces.

Soybeans

Originally from China, most of the soybeans grown in the United States are used for animal feed. As the protein champion of the vegetable kingdom, soybeans are enjoyed by people as sprouts or cooked into soups and casseroles. Soy is also the basis for soy flour, soy milk, miso, tempeh, tofu, soy grits and textured vegetable protein (TVP) meat analogs.

Soy Grits

Soy grits are lightly roasted soybeans which are coarsely cracked. They make a good high-protein meat substitute, or can be added to pancake flour, cereals, casseroles and baked goods.

Sprouts

Fresh sprouts are a healthy, cheap, and versatile food you can grow in your home. Take your pick of alfalfa seeds, mung beans, soybeans and lentils and use them in a variety of salads, sandwiches, stir-fried dishes and soups. For simple sprouting directions, see the recipe section of this book.

Sunflower Seeds

A common bird food, sunflower seeds are enjoying a surge of popularity with people, too. High in protein vitamin B and minerals, they make a hearty snack food (especially with raisins) and are good added to soups, salads and casseroles.

Tabouli See *Bulgur*

Tahini See *Sesame Tahini*

Tamari

Tamari is a fermented form of soy sauce. Though it contains sodium, tamari is high in minerals. Use in place of salt.

Tempeh

Indonesians have enjoyed tempeh for hundreds of years. Made from fermented soybeans, tempeh has more protein than steak and is high in vitamin B-12 and other important nutrients. It is nutritionally superior to tofu. Enjoy tempeh as a main dish in place of chicken or fish.

Tofu

Tofu is a versatile food made from soybeans, and has been considered a staple food in the Orient for thousands of years. Since it takes on the flavor of other foods (it tastes rather bland by itself) high-protein tofu can be enjoyed in stir-fried dishes, dips, spreads, salads, sandwiches, soups, grain dishes, "milk" shakes, and even in desserts such as tofu cream pie. You can bake tofu, fry tofu, boil tofu, or eat it raw with fresh vegetables. It can be kept refrigerated in water for up to two weeks, but remember to change the water daily.

Textured Vegetable Protein (TVP)

Long popular with vegetarians who enjoy the taste and texture of meat, textured vegetable protein is made from wheat or soybeans subjected to a special refining process. The result: A high-protein food similar to red meat, chicken and fish. Used by vegetarians as a main dish and by others who want to lower their cholesterol intake, TVP is also added to meat as a protein extender.

Wakame

A seaweed from Japan, wakame can be enjoyed in soups and stir-fried dishes.

Wheat (Cracked)

When the whole grain of wheat is cracked in processing, you have cracked wheat—a good cereal or rice substitute that contains the same nutritional qualities as whole wheat.

Wheat (Whole)

Whole wheat is what nature intended wheat to be: a complete grain with the bran, germ and vitamins intact. Because it is a complete food, whole wheat contains many important vitamins and trace minerals which cannot always be replaced by "enrichment."

Wheat Germ

Wheat germ is the embryo of the wheat kernel, and is rich in protein, vitamins and minerals. Use it in cereals and to garnish soup, salad and yogurt. Refrigerate to prevent rancidity.

Yogurt

Yogurt has become one of America's most popular health foods. A cultured milk product slightly sour in taste, yogurt is known for its friendly bacteria—the ones which are good for the intestine. The best yogurt is of the unflavored variety, to which you can add fruit, sugarless preserves, wheat germ and nuts. Some preflavored yogurts contain gelatin, sugar, artificial colors and artificial flavors.

Chapter 11

A VEGETARIAN DIET
CAN SAVE YOU MONEY

YOU don't have to be an economist to know how much it costs to feed a family these days. Sporadic food shortages and skyrocketing prices are putting such a strain on the average food budget that many consumers feel that if things don't improve, we'll have to limit our diets to bologna, beans and hamburger.

Meat has long been the leader in the rising cost of food. During the much-publicized United States meat boycott in 1973, millions of Americans stopped eating meat until the prices went down. While many of them returned to their previous diet after the boycott, others discovered something that vegetarians had known for years: A meat-free diet is not only good for your health, but can save you money without sacrificing taste or variety.

In fact a varied, imaginative and healthful vegetarian diet can reduce the average cost of protein from between 25 and 50 percent, and can supply a family with an exciting variety of delicious casseroles, loaves, soups, sandwiches, dips, stews and salads to enjoy.

Vegetarians do not, as is generally supposed, eat

large quantities of expensive vegetables, fruits and nuts. On the contrary, the trend is toward the simpler and less costly foods which can supply most people with more than enough of the recommended nutrients.

Dietitians tell us that the real value of food lies in its nutritional content. The following table compares the general nutritional value of a number of popular foods which are obtained from both animal and plant sources.

Table 11.1

COMPARABLE FOOD VALUES OF EDIBLE PORTIONS, 100 GRAMS

Food	% Water	Grams Protein	Grams Fat	Grams Carbohydrate	Energy Value (Calories)
Beef	66.6	20.2	12.3	0	197
Lamb, loin	59.3	16.8	22.6	0	276
Chicken	75.7	18.6	4.9	0	124
Cheese, swiss	39.0	27.5	28.0	1.7	370
Soybeans (dry, raw)	10.0	34.1	17.7	33.5	403
Lentils (dry, raw)	11.1	24.7	1.1	60.1	340
Chickpeas (dry, raw)	10.7	20.5	4.8	61.0	360
Peanuts	5.6	26.0	47.5	18.6	564
Almonds	4.7	18.6	52.4	19.5	598
Cow's milk (whole, powdered)	2.0	26.4	27.5	38.2	502
Soybean milk (whole, powdered)	4.2	41.8	20.3	28.0	429
Sunflower seeds	4.8	24.0	47.3	19.9	560

Source: *Composition of Foods*

Since meat contains high percentages of water (which you, the consumer, must pay for) and less than a comparable amount of protein, it is obvious that pound for pound, meat is a poor value for the money, especially when compared with high protein vegetarian foods.

How to save money: some concrete suggestions

1. *Buy the inexpensive protein.* The price of protein varies widely among the foods we eat. In fact, some

foods can cost twenty times more than others with the same protein return. By purchasing lower cost protein from nonmeat sources and using them wisely, you can reduce your protein bill from 25 to 50 percent and more. Here are some protein cost comparisons, based on protein food prices in the United States, Canada, and Great Britain.

Table 11.2
COMPARATIVE PROTEIN PRICES

High-Price Proteins	Medium-Price Proteins (save 25%)	Low-Price Proteins (save 50% and more)
Steak	Chicken	Soybeans
Pork chops	Whole milk	Non-fat dry milk
Most fish	Hard cheese	Soy milk powder
Ham	Eggs	Cottage cheese
Frankfurters	Chopped meat	Lentils
Sausage	Wholewheat bread	Most legumes
Almonds	Brown rice	Wholewheat flour
Yogurt	Peanuts	Barley
Sardines	Sunflower seeds	Wheat germ
Pecans	Sesame seeds	Peanut butter
Cold cuts	Chickpeas	Brewer's yeast
Ice cream		Pasta

2. *Combine your proteins.* When certain complementary protein foods are combined, the result is more usable protein for you. In addition to more usable protein per meal, money can be saved as well. The protein foods which complement each other best include rice and legumes, legumes and seeds, rice and dairy products, cornmeal and beans, sesame and legumes, wholewheat and soy, and wholewheat and dairy products.

3. *Shop from a list and not on impulse.* Impulsive buying can destroy a food budget. By carefully planning what you will buy before entering the market, you can save a substantial amount of money. Non-

nutritious convenience foods like food mixes, candy, cookies and sugary drinks are often bought on impulse, and can eliminate any anticipated food savings—even if no meat is purchased. Make a list and follow it.

Some street-wise shoppers suggest that you leave your kids (and perhaps your spouse) at home when you go shopping. They usually want foods you don't need.

An additional suggestion: *Never* go to the market when you're hungry. Hunger is perhaps the best way to lose our objectivity when shopping for what we really need.

4. *Buy food in bulk.* Buying food in bulk reduces packaging and merchandising costs, and the savings are passed on to you. A bulk purchase of vegetarian food can save perhaps an additional 25 percent or more over regular vegetarian savings. Join a neighborhood cooperative, or informally purchase food together with friends or relatives. Divide the large order among yourselves.

Many of the high-protein vegetarian foods can be stored easily and inexpensively for long periods of time. The most easily stored foods are rice, lentils, peas, beans, whole seeds, nuts with shells, soybean and milk powder, whole grains, dry soybean curd (dry tofu), sea vegetables and pasta products.

5. *Avoid the intermediary and save money.* When you buy prepared and highly processed food products, you are paying for many unnecessary extras, with no nutritional return for money spent. Additional labor and machinery expense, unnecessary food additives, fancy packaging, and advertising costs are some of the extras we pay for when we consume such products.

a. Raw food in its natural state is almost always cheaper and more wholesome than processed and elaborately packaged food products. For example, if you spend twelve minutes a week mixing a few pounds of whole–

grain cereal from your choice of grains, seeds, nuts and dried fruits, you can save over 50 percent of the cost of a less exciting, less nutritious commercially prepared cereal. By making a pot of home-made soup, you can save over 80 percent over the cost of canned soups and mixes.

b. Home-baked bread made with wholegrain flour tastes better, remains free of chemical additives, and will cost less than the standard supermarket breads.

c. Sprouting is a simple project you can do indoors. High protein sprouts (from alfalfa seeds, wheat berries, lentils, soybeans and mung beans) taste delicious, are inexpensive, and can be used in many interesting vegetarian dishes. You don't have to buy sprouts in the store. Follow the simple guide to bean sprouting in the recipe section of this book.

d. A garden can supply you with an enormous quantity of wholesome and delicious foods at a small fraction of the often tasteless store-bought variety. For a modest expenditure of money and energy, the returns of a garden are generous indeed.

6. *Especially in the kitchen:* In addition to avoiding the middleman, you can save even more money if you follow a few money-saving tips in the kitchen.

a. Eat salad greens in large pieces rather than shredded to avoid vitamin loss.

b. Soak rice, beans, grains and split peas overnight to cut down on cooking time (and fuel). Large legumes (like chickpeas, navy beans and black-eyed peas) can be prepared in a pressure cooker to save additional energy. However, since split peas and lentils can block the pressure cooking valve if the cooker is overloaded (which is not only messy but dangerous) they should be cooked in smaller quantities or prepared in a regular pot.

c. You can improve the protein content of flour foods by substituting one-fourth soy flour for wholewheat flour. While soy products are generally unavailable in the supermarket (except for canned cooked soybeans, soy sauce and perhaps tofu) you can find soy flour inexpensively at any health food store.

SECTION IV

The Vegetarian Gourmet

Chapter 12

RECIPES FOR LIFE

IF YOU WANT to experience fine vegetarian cuisine, the following recipes are for you. Drawn from a broad spectrum of foods from around the world, they offer variety, good taste and abundant nutrition.

Because pleasurable eating can be healthy as well, our breakfast ideas, main dishes, soups, salads and most desserts are high in protein, low in fat, and offer a bounty of vitamins and minerals. At the same time, sugar, salt and harsh spices have been kept to a minimum. While most recipes do not call for dairy products and eggs, you can add them if you like.

The following easy-to-prepare recipes have been culled from hundreds of sources: friends, relatives, cookbooks and magazines. Some are traditional ethnic favorites which have been enjoyed for hundreds of years. Others are new creations or family secrets that have never been offered "to the public" before. Our breakfast ideas will give you a healthy start each morning, while the fresh salads, hearty soups and high-protein main dishes will keep you going throughout the day. Our desserts provide pleasure without guilt (a rare achievement these days!) while our drinks will leave you both nourished and refreshed.

We hope you will enjoy these recipes and share them with your friends.

Breakfasts———————

BIRCHER MUESLI

8 cups rolled oats
2 cups raisins
1 cup raw wheat germ
½ cup raw sunflower seeds

1 cup chopped raw nuts
    (preferably hazelnuts)
½ cup sesame seeds, toasted

Mix ingredients together in a large bowl. Measure individual serving (1 cup) and place in cereal bowl. Stir in ½ cup hot water, and let stand until water is absorbed (about 5 minutes). Add ½ coarsely grated apple including peel and core. You can also add milk, orange juice, or apple juice instead of water; a tablespoon of yogurt, a teaspoon of good tasting brewer's yeast (by sampling a variety of brands you will find the type most palatable to you) and a dash of cinnamon are nice additions.
Serves 12.

CRUNCHY GRANOLA

8 cups rolled oats
1 cup raw wheat germ
½ cup sesame seeds
1½ cups shredded coconut
½ cup ground raw nuts

½ cup honey
1½ teaspoons sea salt
⅓ cup hot water
½ cup vegetable oil

Mix ingredients together in a large bowl. Spread the mixture across the bottom of a baking sheet or pan. Bake at 350° for about 35 minutes, or until granola turns golden brown. Stir twice so that everything toasts evenly.
Serves 4 people for a week.

WHOLEWHEAT PANCAKE MIX

3 cups wholewheat flour
1 cup soy flour
1 cup buckwheat flour
1 cup wheat germ

½ cup undegerminated
    cornmeal
¼ cup brewer's yeast
¼ cup powdered lecithin

Keep in a cool place in a tightly closed container.
To make pancakes:

1 cup pancake mix
½ teaspoon baking powder
2 tablespoons oil

2 eggs (optional)
1 cup milk (animal or soy)
½ cup raisins

Mix the dry ingredients together. Beat eggs, if used, with milk and add to dry mixture. Add raisins. Cook on hot oiled griddle.
Serves 4.

ECUADOREAN POTATO PANCAKES
(Llapingachos)

2 cups boiled potatoes
½ cup tofu, diced
½ cup cooked brown rice
1 medium onion, chopped
1 small red pepper, chopped

2 tablespoons parsley, chopped
2 tablespoons oil
salt and pepper to taste

Dice the potatoes and combine with the other ingredients. Form individual patties and cook on hot griddle. Cook slowly until well browned.
Serves 4.

SCRAMBLED TOFU

1 medium onion, diced
2 tablespoons oil
1 pound tofu, crumbled
6 mushrooms, sliced

1 clove garlic, minced
salt and pepper to taste
1 teaspoon soy sauce

Fry the onion in oil until golden. Add the tofu, mushrooms, garlic and seasonings. Cook for 5 minutes, stirring often. Add the soy sauce. Season. Serve as an entree with rice or noodles, or serve over wholegrain toast with ketchup or mustard.
Serves 2.

LEONITA'S CORN-BUCKWHEAT BREAD
Great with breakfast!

¾ cup cornmeal
½ cup buckwheat flour
½ cup buckwheat groats
   (kasha)
2 teaspoons baking powder
2 teaspoons ground ginger
1 teaspoon cinnamon

¾ cup sunflower seeds, hulled
½ cup soy powder
1 cup apple juice or water
1 tablespoon molasses
1 tablespoon honey or barley
   malt

Preheat oven to 350°. Grease oblong dish or two pie plates with oil. Combine all dry ingredients (except the soy powder) in a large bowl. Mix well. Place soy powder and juice (or water) in blender with the molasses and honey or barley malt. Blend briefly and add to dry ingredients. Pour into greased plates and bake for 30 minutes. Cool on rack and cut into squares or wedges. Serves 4 easily.

Soups _____

LENTIL-RICE-TOMATO SOUP

1 medium onion, chopped
2 tablespoons oil
1 cup dry lentils
½ cup brown rice
6 cups water

1 pound tomatoes (fresh or
   canned), diced
1 cup tomato sauce or puree
pinch of sweet basil
salt and pepper to taste

Sauté the onion in oil until golden (not brown). Add the lentils and rice. Add the water and bring to a boil. Cook over low heat until the lentils and rice are done. Add the tomatoes (whole and sauce), sweet basil and seasoning. Heat before serving.
Serves 6.

SOYBEAN VEGETABLE SOUP

1 cup dry soybeans
6½ cups water
1 pound tomatoes
1 cup celery, sliced
1 cup carrots, diced
1 cup potatoes, diced

2 cloves garlic, minced
3 teaspoons vegetable bouillon
   powder
1 bay leaf
salt and pepper to taste
1 cup mushrooms

Soak soybeans overnight in 3 cups of water. Discard water. Add remaining 3½ cups of water, cover, and cook slowly for about 2 hours. Add vegetables (except the mushrooms) and seasonings. Cover and cook slowly for about 35 minutes, or until vegetables are tender. At this point, add the mushrooms and cook for another 5 minutes. Remove bay leaf before serving.
Serves 6.

HEARTY VEGETARIAN VEGETABLE SOUP

3 stalks celery, sliced
2 medium onions, chopped
2 tablespoons vegetable oil
2 quarts water
2 large potatoes, cubed
2 large carrots, diced
¼ cup barley

¼ cup brown rice
3 medium tomatoes, cubed
1 cup peas, corn, beans
¼ cup parsley
4 tablespoons vegetable bouillon powder
½ cup mushrooms, sliced

Brown the celery and onions in oil. Add water, vegetables (except the mushrooms) and other ingredients. Season to taste. Cook until it is almost to your liking; add the mushrooms and cook for a few minutes until done.
Serves 8.

POTATO MUSHROOM SOUP

2 large potatoes, peeled and cubed
2 medium onions, diced
6 stalks celery, coarsely chopped
4 cups water

½ pound mushrooms, quartered
½ pound tofu, diced
1 cup milk (animal or soy)
2 tablespoons soy sauce
pepper to taste

Boil the potatoes, onions and celery in the water until potatoes are tender. Add the mushrooms, tofu, milk and seasonings. Simmer for 5 more minutes.
Serves 6.

AHIMSA PEA SOUP

2 cups split peas
2 carrots, diced
1 large potato, grated
2 stalks celery, sliced
2 onions, cubed
1 tablespoon parsley

2 quarts water
4 tablespoons vegetable bouillon powder base
6 cloves
dash cayenne pepper

Combine the ingredients and cook until peas are soft. Season to taste. Top with finely chopped raw onion or scallions.
Serves 8.

LUXEMBOURG NAVY BEAN SOUP

1 cup dried navy beans
6 cups water
2 medium potatoes, diced

1 large leek, chopped
2 jiggers of wine or sherry
salt and pepper to taste

Pour the water over the beans and soak overnight. The following morning, bring beans to a boil and cook for two hours or until soft. Add water as soup thickens. Add the potatoes and leek. Cook for another 20 minutes, or until potatoes are soft. Add sherry just before serving. Tradition calls for a dish of stewed prunes to be served alongside.
Serves 6.

LIMA BEAN SOUP

1 cup dry lima beans
2 quarts water
2 medium onions, chopped

1 clove garlic, minced
1 cup corn
salt and pepper to taste

Soak beans overnight in the water. Cook for one hour or until they are tender. Sauté the onions until they are soft. Add the garlic and corn. Add to the lima beans, using more water if necessary. Season to taste.
Serves 8.

MEXICAN CHICKPEA-CORN SOUP

2 onions, diced
2 cups cooked chickpeas (garbanzo beans)
2 cups sweet corn
8 cups water
½ cup tomato puree
½ pound mushrooms, sliced
½ teaspoon chili pepper
   (optional)
salt and pepper to taste

Brown the onion in oil in a large pot. Add the other ingredients. Boil for about 15 minutes and serve. Garnish with finely chopped scallions or raw onion.
Serves 8.

TAHINI NOODLE SOUP

½ pound wholewheat noodles
6 cups water
2 scallions, chopped
½ pound tofu, cubed
½ teaspoon kelp powder
½ cup dried kelp or wakame,
   cut into ½" pieces
5 tablespoons sesame tahini
4 tablespoons miso

Cook the noodles in water for about five minutes and add the scallions, tofu, kelp powder and sea vegetables. Cook until the noodles are tender. Remove ½ cup of broth and dissolve the tahini and miso. Turn off flame, stir into soup. Season to taste.
Serves 4 to 6.

Salads and Dressings ____

GREEK SALAD WITH TOFU

2 medium kirby cucumbers*
2 large, ripe tomatoes
2-3 scallions
1 medium green pepper
1 cup fresh alfalfa sprouts
½ pound tofu
soy sauce to taste
cracked green olives (to taste)
1 clove garlic, minced

Cut up the cucumbers, tomatoes, scallions and pepper into small pieces. Add the sprouts. Crumble the tofu over the salad. Sprinkle with soy sauce, and garnish with olives and garlic.

*the tiny cucumbers used in making pickles.
Serves 2.

SPINACH NOODLE SALAD

½ pound spinach noodles
1 tablespoon smooth unsalted peanut butter
3 tablespoons soy sauce
4 tablespoons rice vinegar
4 tablespoons Oriental sesame oil (available in Oriental food stores)
1 teaspoon ginger, minced (fresh ginger root if possible)
1 clove garlic, minced
3 scallions, finely chopped

Cook the noodles in boiling water until tender. Drain and rinse in cold water. Let stand in serving bowl. Combine the peanut butter and soy sauce, and mix until peanut butter is dissolved. Add the vinegar, sesame oil, ginger, garlic and half the scallions and toss well. Sprinkle with the remaining scallions and serve.
Serves 4.

COLOMBIAN BEAN SALAD

1 pound cooked pinto beans, rinsed
juice of half a lemon
3 teaspoons oil
½ teaspoon soy sauce
pepper to taste
⅛ teaspoon powdered mustard seed
1 clove garlic, finely chopped
several lettuce leaves
2 medium tomatoes, sliced
1 onion, sliced into rings

Mix the beans with the lemon juice, oil, soy sauce, pepper and mustard. Top with garlic and decorate with lettuce, tomatoes and onion rings. Add the seasoning.
Serves 4.

OVERSTUFFED TOMATOES

4 *large ripe tomatoes*
1 *large ripe avocado,*
 peeled, seeded and mashed
2 *scallions, chopped*

1 *medium green pepper,*
 chopped
romaine lettuce

Slice the tops off the tomatoes and scoop out the inside carefully. Mix with avocado, scallions and green pepper. Stuff into the tomato skins and serve on a bed of crisp romaine.
Serves 4.

TABOULI SALAD

1 *cup bulgur*
1 *teaspoon mint leaves,*
 chopped fine
1 *cup fresh parsley,*
 chopped fine
4 *medium ripe tomatoes,*

 coarsely chopped
1 *bunch scallions, chopped*
¼ *cup lemon juice*
1 *teaspoon cinnamon*
¼ *cup olive oil*
salt and pepper to taste

Soak bulgur in water to cover for at least one hour or until completely expanded. After soaking, squeeze out excess water. Mix bulgur with the mint, parsley, tomatoes and scallions. Add the lemon juice, cinnamon and oil. Salt and pepper to taste. Serve chilled.
Serves 4.

IRISH SALAD

2 *cups cold mashed*
 potatoes
½ *cup tofu, diced*
2 *tablespoons parsley,*

 chopped
1 *medium onion, diced*
1½ *tablespoons vinegar*
salt and pepper to taste

Mix potatoes together with the other ingredients. When ready to serve, shape into small balls and place on lettuce leaves. Serve cold with your choice of dressing.
Serves 4.

LIMA BEAN SALAD

2 *cups baby lima beans,*
  cooked
1 *cup celery, diced*
1 *large onion, sliced*
2 *scallions, sliced*

2 *or 3 large ripe tomatoes,*
  sliced
1 *green pepper, sliced*
salt and pepper to taste

Mix lima beans, celery, onion and scallions. Add seasonings. Marinate in the dressing of your choice (vinegar and oil or French dressing are recommended). Arrange tomato slices around a bed of lettuce and place bean mixture in the center. Garnish with pepper slices. Serve with wholegrain bread sticks or crackers.
Serves 6.

TOFU GUACAMOLE

1 *large ripe avocado*
1 *pound tofu*
3 *tablespoons oil*
1 *onion, chopped*
1 *tomato, diced*

1 *clove garlic, minced*
1 *teaspoon lemon juice*
1 *teaspoon soy sauce*
pinch cayenne
salt and pepper to taste

Mash the avocado and tofu, and add the other ingredients. Mix well. Serve on wholegrain bread, in tacos, or as a dip with vegetable slices or corn chips.
Serves 4.

SPROUTS
(Alfalfa, mung, soy, lentil, garbanzo)

Wash 2 tablespoons of seeds or beans
Soak in wide-mouthed 1-quart jar
   -6 hours for alfalfa seeds or wheat berries
   -9 hours for soybeans or garbanzo beans
   -16 hours for lentils or mung beans

Drain off water. Cover jar loosely with cheesecloth or

nylon netting and keep in a dark warm (72°) place. Rinse seeds or beans three times a day. Drain. After three days (or when sprouts are at least an inch long) they are ready to eat. Larger amounts can be made in larger containers. Enjoy sprouted seeds and beans in sandwiches, soups, salads and stir-fried dishes.

CURRIED TOFU RICE SALAD

1 pound tofu, cut into small pieces
2½ cups cooked, chilled brown rice
1 medium onion, minced
2 tablespoons parsley, minced
2 medium green peppers: one cut into slivers; one sliced into rings
2 tomatoes, cut into wedges
lettuce leaves

Mix first four ingredients together. Serve on lettuce leaves and decorate with tomatoes and peppers.

Dressing:

6 tablespoons oil
1 teaspoon curry powder
2 tablespoons lemon juice
1 clove garlic, minced
2 tablespoons soy sauce

Mix together and pour over salad.
Serves 2 generously.

BEET DRESSING

1 cup safflower or olive oil
juice of 1 lemon
1 beet, chopped
1 clove garlic, chopped
2 tablespoons soy sauce
¼ cup water

Combine ingredients in blender. Pour over salad.

SESAME DRESSING

½ cup sesame tahini
2 tablespoons toasted
   sesame seeds
2 cloves garlic
1 apple, peeled and cored

1 cup water
¼ cup lemon juice
apple cider vinegar (to
   taste)
2 tablespoons soy sauce

Blend in blender. If mixture is too thick, add more water. Great over romaine lettuce, cucumber salad, and with brown rice and rye berries. Perfect topping for the Gazebo sandwich (see recipe).

CREAMY SCALLION DRESSING

½ pound tofu
2 scallions, chopped
2 tablespoons lemon juice

2 teaspoons oil
2 teaspoons soy sauce
salt and pepper to taste

Mix all ingredients together in a blender. Add water if needed.

CREAMY TOFU DRESSING

6 ounces tofu, well drained
2 tablespoons oil
2 tablespoons minced onion

2 tablespoons lemon juice
2 tablespoons soy sauce
½ teaspoon curry powder

Combine ingredients in a blender and puree. If refrigerated, this dressing will keep for three days.

SPICY FRENCH DRESSING

1½ cups oil
1 clove garlic, minced
3 tablespoons grated onion
1 tablespoon prepared
   mustard

2 tablespoons soy sauce
⅓ cup vinegar
1 tablespoon lemon juice
1 cup tomato sauce

Mix all ingredients together. Chill. Makes about 3 cups of dressing.

*Sandwich Fixings*_____

HUMMUS

1 cup onion, chopped
1 clove garlic, chopped
1 cup garbanzos
  (chickpeas)
¼ cup lemon juice

¼ cup oil
¼ cup tahini
handful sesame seeds
salt to taste

Sauté onions and garlic. Place chickpeas in blender, and blend with juice, oil, and sautéed onions and garlic until smooth. (You may have to add more juice or chickpeas to reach proper consistency.) Add tahini, sesame seeds and season to taste.
For 4 portions.

FELAFEL

3 cups cooked garbanzo
  beans (chickpeas)
1 medium potato, cooked
  and mashed
2 small onions, finely
  chopped
⅓ cup wholewheat bread
  crumbs

2 cloves garlic, minced
¼ cup sesame tahini
juice of 1 lemon
1 teaspoon paprika
1 tablespoon parsley, finely
  chopped
⅛ teaspoon pepper
salt to taste

Blend the garbanzos with the mashed potatoes and form a paste. Sauté the onions until soft. Add the garbanzos and potatoes, bread crumbs, garlic, tahini, lemon juice and seasonings. Mix well. Mixture should be a bit on the soft side. Form into small balls (about an inch in diameter) and place on a lightly oiled tray. Place in 350° oven and bake for 10 minutes.
Serve in a pita bread with chopped lettuce, tomatoes and onions, topped with sesame herb dressing (see recipe).
Makes about 24.

SOYBEAN BURGERS

2 cups soybeans, cooked
1 medium onion, chopped
¾ cup wheat germ
1 carrot, grated
2 eggs (or 2 tablespoons

arrowroot powder)
½ teaspoon ground dill
3 tablespoons dried
   parsley
salt and pepper to taste

Mix all ingredients together and form into patties. Fry in a small amount of oil until golden brown. Lentils, chickpeas or navy beans can be substituted for soybeans. **Serves 6.**

GAZEBO SANDWICH

½ cup tabouli (see recipe)
2 pitas (Middle Eastern
   flatbread)
2 tablespoons cottage
   cheese (or diced tofu)
2 lettuce leaves, chopped
4 cucumber slices

1 shredded carrot
1 shredded beet
¼ cup sunflower seeds,
   hulled
sesame herb dressing (see
   recipe)

Place the tabouli in the pita bread, followed by the cottage cheese or tofu. Add the vegetables one by one and sprinkle with sunflower seeds. Top the sandwich with dressing. **Serves 2.**

CUBAN BLACK BEAN SPREAD

1 cup cooked black beans
⅓ cup sesame tahini
2 cloves garlic, minced
2 tablespoons lemon juice
½ teaspoon salt or soy

sauce
handful sesame seeds
dash cayenne pepper
fresh parsley, chopped

Place all ingredients (except the parsley) into blender and blend until smooth. Place in a bowl and garnish with lots of chopped parsley. Serve as a spread for thin crackers, as a sandwich, or a dip. Adequate for 4. (Kidney beans can be substituted for black beans.)

PEANUT BUTTER SANDWICH SUPRÊME

Take several tablespoons of unhydrogenated peanut butter (homemade or the health food store variety) and mix with a few hulled sunflower seeds. Spread liberally over wholegrain bread and top with ripe banana slices. Delicious!

EASY BEAN SPREAD

Take leftover navy beans (or other dark or light beans) and mash. Add ketchup, miso, hot sauce or pepper if desired. Mix with finely chopped onions for a super sandwich spread. Top your sandwich with sliced cucumbers, alfalfa sprouts or tomato slices.

Main Dishes ———————

VEGETARIAN CHILI

½ pound dry kidney beans
6 cups water
2 large onions, chopped
4 stalks celery, chopped
2 cloves garlic, minced

½ pound tomatoes (canned
*   or fresh), cut into*
*   pieces*
½ teaspoon chili powder
salt and pepper to taste

Soak beans overnight in 6 cups water and cook until nearly done. Sauté onions, celery and garlic. Add to beans. Add the tomatoes and seasonings. Cook until vegetables are done. Serve with finely chopped onion over rice.
Serves 6.

BRAZILIAN FEIJAO

1 pound dry black beans
6 cups water
3 medium onions, chopped
1 large tomato, diced (or
    ½ pound canned tomato
    pieces)
1 bay leaf
1 teaspoon black pepper

or pinch of cayenne
4 tablespoons soy sauce
4 scallions, chopped
6 cloves garlic, chopped
    (use less if you're not
    adventurous!)
salt to taste

Soak beans overnight in water to cover. Cook for 90 minutes until tender. After an hour of cooking add half the onions, the tomato, bay leaf, pepper and soy sauce. In a frying pan sauté the remaining onions, scallions and garlic. Salt and pepper to taste. Add to beans just before serving. Serve over bed of brown rice. Maravilha! Serves 6.

NAVY BEAN STEW

1½ cups dry navy beans
5 cups water
1 large onion, chopped
2 medium carrots, sliced
2 stalks celery, chopped
¼ cup kelp, cut into ½"
    pieces (optional)
¼ teaspoon dry mustard

2 cloves garlic, minced
2 tablespoons soy sauce
1 teaspoon dried parsley
¼ teaspoon thyme
pepper to taste
⅓ cup wholewheat
    flour

Soak the beans overnight in the 5 cups of water. Bring to a boil, reduce heat and cook, covered, for 1 hour. Add the onion, carrot, celery, kelp and seasonings. Stir in the flour slowly, to prevent lumping, and continue cooking for 30 minutes more or until the beans are tender.

Serve garnished with finely chopped raw onion or scallions.

Serves 6.

BEANPOT WITH OREGANO

1 cup dry pink beans
⅓ cup dry navy beans
½ cup dry black beans
6 cups water
½ cup uncooked brown rice
1 medium onion, chopped
1 medium green pepper,
   chopped
4 carrots, sliced
3 tablespoons oil
½ pound mushrooms,
   quartered
2 tablespoons honey
1 teaspoon salt
¼ teaspoon pepper
½ teaspoon oregano
¼ teaspoon dried chili
   peppers, ground
wholewheat bread crumbs
½ cup chopped fresh
   parsley

Soak beans in the water overnight. Cook together with rice for 90 minutes. Sauté onion, green pepper, and carrots in oil. Cook 5 minutes. (Don't cook the mushrooms or parsley.)
Add the mushrooms, honey and seasonings and place in casserole. Top with wholewheat breadcrumbs. If mixture becomes dry, add ½ cup liquid.
Bake for 30 minutes at 325°.
Garnish with the parsley.
Serves 4.

CURRIED CHICKPEA DINNER

2 large onions, chopped
1 medium green pepper,
   chopped
2 cloves garlic, minced
oil
2 cups cooked chickpeas
dash curry powder
dash turmeric
2 cups cooked brown rice
salt and pepper to taste

Sauté onions, green pepper and garlic in oil until browned. Add chickpeas, curry powder, turmeric and small amount of water. Add the brown rice. Cover and cook for about ten minutes.
Serve with steamed asparagus or spinach.
Serves 6 to 8.

CHICKPEA-VEGETABLE CASSEROLE

2 medium zucchini, sliced
2 medium onions, sliced
½ medium eggplant, cut
  into pieces
1 green pepper, sliced
1 cup mushrooms,
  quartered

oil
1 cup cooked chickpeas
2 medium potatoes, sliced
1 cup tomato sauce
2 tablespoons lemon juice
bread crumbs
salt and pepper to taste

Cook each vegetable except the chickpeas and potatoes
separately in oil. (Boil the potatoes until nearly done,
slice, and then bake until golden brown.)
Mix all ingredients together in large bowl. Place mixture in oiled, breaded casserole. Sprinkle more bread
crumbs over the mixture. Place in 350° oven for 20 to 30
minutes.
Serve with brown rice or barley.
Serves 6.

CHICKPEA-ZUCCHINI CASSEROLE

3 cups cooked chickpeas,
  drained
2 medium onions, coarsely
  chopped
1 large clove garlic, finely
  minced
2 pounds tomatoes,
  chopped (fresh or canned
  with liquid)
1 teaspoon tahini

2 teaspoons ground
  coriander
¾ teaspoon ground cumin
¼ teaspoon ground allspice
pepper to taste
2 pounds slim, young
  zucchini, sliced
chopped walnuts to taste
black olives to taste

Place the chickpeas in a casserole dish.
In a saucepan, sauté the onions, garlic, tomatoes and
seasonings. Pour over chickpeas. Add the raw zucchini.

Bake in a 400° oven, covered, for 30 minutes. Uncover and bake for another 20 minutes until juices are thickened and bubbling.

Remove from oven and garnish with walnuts and olives.
Serves 6.

FAVA BEANS ITALIANO

2 green peppers, chopped
1 medium onion, chopped
4 cloves garlic, minced
6 tablespoons oil
3 cups cooked fava beans
4 medium zucchini, diced

1 cup fresh mushrooms,
   quartered
2 teaspoons basil leaves
2 dried hot red peppers
   with seeds removed,
   chopped fine

Sauté peppers, onion and garlic in oil. Combine all ingredients including seasoning. Bake for 30 minutes at 350° in covered casserole dish. Cover surface with grated cheese or diced tofu.
Serves 4.

FAVA BEANS WITH PEPPERS

2 large onions, chopped
3 pounds bell peppers,
   sliced
1 pound tofu, diced

oil
salt and pepper to taste
1 cup cooked fava beans

Sauté the onions, peppers and tofu. Add the seasonings and some oil. Add the beans.

Cover saucepan and cook for 20 minutes over medium flame.

Serve over rice.

Garbanzo beans may be used in place of the fava beans.
Serves 6.

CURRIED RICE AND LENTILS

1 large onion, finely
  chopped
1 large apple; peeled,
  cored and finely chopped or
  grated
¼ cup oil
3 cloves garlic, minced

1-2 teaspoons curry powder
⅔ cup water
1 tablespoon honey
4 cups cooked lentils
2 cups cooked brown rice
salt and pepper to taste

Sauté the onion and apple in oil until soft. Add garlic and curry powder and continue to sauté for 5 minutes. Add water and honey, and simmer in covered pan until mixture is well blended.
Add the lentils and rice and season to taste.
Serves 4 to 5.

ORIENTAL LENTILS

1 large onion, chopped
1 clove garlic, minced
2 tablespoons oil
6 ground cardamon seeds
2 cups cooked lentils

½ teaspoon miso (dissolved in
  2 teaspoons water)
juice of ½ lemon
2 cups cooked brown rice

Fry the onion and garlic until they turn a golden brown. Add the cardamon seeds and lentils and cook for 5 minutes. Season to taste, adding the lemon juice and miso. Serve over a bed of brown rice.
Serves 4.

THANKSGIVING LENTIL-NUT RING

2 cups cooked lentils
½ cup milk (animal or soy)
  or tomato puree
2 tablespoons oil
1½ cups dry wholewheat
  bread crumbs
2 tablespoons soy flour
1 cup walnuts, chopped
1 medium onion, finely

chopped
1 cup grated carrots
1 cup celery, finely chopped
1 teaspoon sage
1 teaspoon thyme, rosemary
  or marjoram
½ teaspoon oregano
salt and pepper to taste
fine bread crumbs

Combine all the ingredients and mix well.

Oil a ring mold (or loaf pan) and sprinkle bottom and sides with fine bread crumbs.

Add lentil mixture and bake at 350° for 90 minutes. Let sit 5 to 10 minutes before unmolding.

Unmold on serving platter; fill center with cooked peas or carrots if desired and garnish with fresh chopped parsley.

Serve in slices with tomato sauce or brown gravy (see recipe) and cranberry sauce.

Serves 8.

BROWN GRAVY

4 tablespoons wholewheat
   flour
2 cups cold water
½ teaspoon salt
¼ teaspoon onion salt
¼ teaspoon garlic salt

1 tablespoon onion,
   minced
2 teaspoons soy sauce
1 teaspoon vegetable
   bouillon powder

Combine flour and water and stir until blended. Cook over low heat until thick. Add remaining ingredients and cook over low flame for 5 to 10 minutes, stirring often.

PEPPERS STUFFED WITH BEANS

½ pound pink beans
6 cups water
1 onion chopped
¼ cup oil
½ cup tomato puree
3 ounces tofu, cut into ¼"
   cubes
⅓ cup cream or soy milk

½ teaspoon oregano
salt and pepper to taste
4 large green peppers
tomato juice
Optional: ⅓ cup each of
   chopped onions, tomatoes
   and carrots

Soak beans overnight in 6 cups water and then cook until soft. Drain and mash. Brown the onion in 2 tablespoons of oil, and add the mashed beans and sauté.

Add the tomato puree, tofu, cream, oregano and seasoning.

Clean and core the peppers. Stuff sautéed ingredients into peppers. Grease and crumb casserole. Add ½" tomato juice and a layer of chopped onions, tomato and carrots mixed, if desired.

Set peppers atop this layer. Sprinkle with wheat germ or grated cheese.

Bake for 25 minutes in 350° oven. Serve with brown rice.

Serves 4.

SHEPHERD'S PIE

1½ cups vegetable bouillon
2 large carrots, diced
2 cups cooked Great
    Northern beans
2 medium onions, sliced
¼ cup wholewheat flour
3 tablespoons oil

½ teaspoon salt or soy
    sauce
1 teaspoon marjoram
⅛ teaspoon pepper
3 cups hot mashed
    potatoes, seasoned to taste

Heat the vegetable bouillon to boiling. Add the carrots and beans. Cover and cook until carrots are tender (about 20 minutes).

Drain. Save liquid. Add water if needed to make 2 cups. Preheat oven to 400°.

Place beans, carrots, and onions in 2-quart baking dish.

Cook flour in oil until it is lightly browned.

Add seasonings and stir in the 2 cups liquid. Cook, stirring constantly, until thickened. Pour sauce over vegetables.

Spread the mashed potatoes over the vegetables.

Bake 15-20 minutes or until potatoes are golden brown.

Serves 6.

PASTA E FAGIOLI

½ pound dry pinto beans
6 cups water
3 medium onions, chopped
¼ cup oil
1 tablespoon soy sauce
1 pound cored, blended

tomatoes (or 1 pound can)
¼ cup dry kelp or kombu,
   cut into ½" pieces (optional)
2 cloves garlic
1 pound wholewheat or
   artichoke spaghetti

Soak beans overnight in 6 cups water. Cook until soft.
Fry the onions in the oil and soy sauce. Add tomatoes,
kelp, garlic and seasoning. Mix well.
Cook the spaghetti according to directions. Drain and
combine with other ingredients.
Serve with tossed salad, breadsticks and a green cooked
vegetable.
Serves 6.

WHOLEWHEAT SPAGHETTI PRIMAVERA

2 quarts water, salted
1 cup fresh shelled green
   peas
2 cups broccoli flowerets
2 medium zucchini, cubed
2 tablespoons oil
1 medium onion, chopped
2 cloves garlic, minced
2 medium tomatoes,
   chopped

½ cup dry white wine
½ teaspoon dried basil
½ pound tofu blended in ½
   cup water
soy sauce and pepper to
   taste
1 pound wholewheat
   spaghetti
grated Parmesan cheese
   (optional)

Bring 2 quarts salted water to a boil. Add the peas and
cook for 5 minutes. Add the broccoli and zucchini and
cook another 2 minutes. Drain.
Sauté the onion and garlic in oil until tender. Add the
tomatoes and sauté another 3 minutes. Add the wine
and basil and cook for 5 minutes.
Stir in the tofu cream and cook over medium heat for 3
minutes. Season to taste and remove from heat.
Meanwhile, cook the spaghetti until tender. Drain.

Pour the sauce over spaghetti, toss and serve with grated Parmesan cheese, if desired.
Serves 4.

LOU ANN'S SPECIAL SPAGHETTI DINNER

1 pound spaghetti (artichoke or wholewheat)
2 large onions, chopped
1 medium green pepper, chopped
2 cloves garlic, chopped oil
1 cup green lima beans (fresh or frozen)
2 large tomatoes, cubed
½ pound tofu, cubed

2 small, thin zucchini, sliced
¼ pound mushrooms, quartered
1 pint tomato sauce
¼ cup dry kelp, cut into ½" strips (optional)
oregano and pepper to taste
3 basil leaves
grated Parmesan cheese or diced tofu

Cook spaghetti until just tender (do not overcook). Drain and rinse. Sauté onions, green pepper and garlic in a small amount of oil. When tender, add lima beans, tomatoes, tofu and zucchini. Cover and cook for 3 to 5 minutes.
Add mushrooms, tomato sauce and seasonings. Simmer.
Pour over spaghetti. Add grated cheese or tofu if desired.
Serve with fresh green salad, bread or breadsticks and fresh fruit.
Serves 4.

WHOLEWHEAT FETTUCCINE WITH MUSHROOMS

4 tablespoons oil
¾ pound fresh mushrooms, sliced
2 cloves garlic, minced
½ pound wholewheat

fettuccine
½ cup vegetable stock
salt and pepper to taste
freshly grated Parmesan cheese or finely diced tofu

Sauté mushrooms and garlic together in 2 tablespoons

of oil in pan. Remove from heat. Cook the fettuccine in water until tender. Reheat the mushrooms and garlic and add seasonings.

Drain fettuccine and transfer to warm serving bowl. Toss with the mushrooms. Add remaining oil and stock to the skillet and cook over high heat for a couple of minutes. Pour over the noodles and mushrooms and toss lightly. Serve at once with Parmesan cheese or diced tofu.

Serves 2 to 3.

PAELLA VEGETARIANA

6 tablespoons oil
2 cloves garlic, chopped
2 medium onions, chopped
2 medium tomatoes, cut
　into eighths
1 pound tofu, diced
1 sweet red pepper, diced
1 green pepper, sliced
1 medium eggplant, cubed

1 cup tender green peas
¼ cup sliced olives
2 cups half-cooked brown
　rice
1 cup water
½ pound fresh mushrooms,
　halved
pinch of saffron
salt and pepper to taste

Use a large heavy pan you can bring to the table. Heat the oil and sauté the garlic and onions for five minutes. Add the tomatoes, tofu, peppers, eggplant, peas and olives and sauté for another few minutes. Add the rice and continue stirring.

Pour in one cup of water and continue cooking until rice is almost done.

At this point, add the mushrooms and continue to cook until rice is tender (rather than sticky).

Dissolve the saffron in a teaspoon of hot water and stir in before serving.

Serves 6.

SALVADOREAN BAKED RICE

1 large onion, diced
1 potato, cubed
6 pitted olives
1 large ripe tomato, diced
1 green pepper, diced

1 cup brown rice, cooked
1 pound tofu, cut into blocks
¼ cup wheat germ or grated
  cheese
salt and pepper to taste

Fry the onion and potato until brown and the potato is
cooked. Add the olives, tomato and pepper and cook for
five minutes.
Add rice and tofu.
Place in oiled casserole dish.
Sprinkle with wheat germ or grated cheese.
Bake 15 to 20 minutes at 350°.
Serves 4.

CASHEW NUTS AND RAISINS PULAO

¼ cup vegetable oil
1½ cups raw brown rice
2 onions, diced
½ cup cashews, chopped
½ cup raisins

2 eggs, slightly beaten or 2
  tablespoons arrowroot
  powder
3 cups water
salt to taste

Heat oil in a large pot. Add the rice and onions, and
cook for one minute. Add the other ingredients along
with the water. Cook for 45 minutes.
Serves 6.

MILLET WITH VEGETABLES

2 carrots, diced
1 stalk celery, diced
1 cup spinach, chopped
1 medium onion, sliced
1 cup green peas
2 tablespoons oil
1 cup dry millet

½ teaspoon dry rosemary
2 cups vegetable broth or
  water
1 tablespoon butter or
  margarine
1 tablespoon grated cheese
salt and pepper to taste

Sauté the vegetables together in oil with the millet and
rosemary. Stir frequently.

Add boiling water or broth and cook over medium flame for 20 minutes. Just before serving, blend in the butter and/or cheese and seasoning if desired.
Serves 4.

OATCAKES WITH
VEGETABLES ARCHAMBAULT

2 small onions, chopped
2 leeks, chopped
1 stalk celery, chopped
4 leaves spinach, chopped
2 carrots, grated
1 tablespoon vegetable oil

1 cup boiling water
1 cup rolled oats
salt and pepper to taste
1 egg (or 1 tablespoon
   arrowroot powder)

Brown the vegetables together in a saucepan with oil. Pour in the water, and add the oats. Add more water if mixture is too thick.
Cook for 10 to 15 minutes until a puree is obtained. Sprinkle with salt and pepper.
Form into patties by hand, and soak patties briefly in egg or arrowroot-water mixture.
Cook in frying pan until golden brown.
Serves 4.

SAN FRANCISCO PILAF

¼ cup oil
1 cup celery, chopped
6 medium onions, sliced
   fine
2 cups bulgur or brown
   rice
2 cups vegetable broth

2 cups boiling water
1 cup almonds or
   cashews, chopped
1½ teaspoon salt
¼ teaspoon marjoram
½ teaspoon oregano

Brown the celery and onions in oil, and add the bulgur and brown.
Place in a 2-quart casserole and pour the broth and boiling water on top.

Blend in the almonds, salt, marjoram and oregano.
Cover and bake in a 325° oven for 90 minutes.
Serves 8.

BARLEY PILAF

2 *medium onions, chopped*
2 *tablespoons oil*
1 *cup barley*
2 *cups boiling water*
½ *pound tofu, cubed*
1 *cup fresh mushrooms,*

quartered
3 *pimentos, chopped*
1 *cup vegetable stock*
1 *teaspoon salt*
⅛ *teaspoon pepper*

Brown the onions in 2 tablespoons oil. Add the barley
and cover with boiling water. Place over low fire to
steam. Steam for 25 minutes (steaming time depends
on type of barley used). Place in casserole dish and add
the tofu, mushrooms, pimentos, vegetable stock, salt
and pepper.
Cover and bake for 30 minutes at 350°.
Serves 4.

SADIE'S STUFFED PEPPERS

4 *large green peppers*
1 *medium onion, chopped*
1 *stalk celery, diced*
2 *tablespoons vegetable*
   oil
1 *cup brown rice, cooked*
1 *cup barley, cooked*

2 *tablespoons parsley*
1 *teaspoon salt*
½ *teaspoon pepper*
1 *teaspoon basil*
1 *cup tomato sauce*
wheat germ

Cut tops from peppers and remove the seeds (which
you can save for next year's garden). Set aside. Sauté
the onion, celery and tops of peppers, except for stem,
(which you have chopped) in oil until tender.
Add brown rice and barley, along with the seasonings.
Mix well. Spoon ¼ cup of the tomato sauce into
casserole dish. Fill the peppers with the mixture, and

place in casserole. Cover peppers with remaining tomato
sauce and sprinkle with wheat germ.
Bake for 30 minutes in 350° oven.
Serves 4.

STUFFED TOMATOES

6 large, ripe, firm tomatoes
1 large onion, finely
  chopped
⅓ cup olive oil
1 cup cooked brown rice
¼ cup pine nuts (or other
  nuts, chopped)
¼ cup fresh parsley,

finely chopped
¼ cup wheat germ
¼ teaspoon ground
  coriander
1 tablespoon dried dill weed
salt and pepper to taste
⅓ cup vegetable broth or
  water

Slice the cap off the stem end of the tomatoes, and
scoop out the pulp. Turn tomatoes upside down to
drain. Sauté the onion in 3 tablespoons of oil until
soft. Remove from heat and blend with the leftover
tomato pulp and other ingredients (except liquid).
Fill tomatoes ¾ full with the mixture. Cover with the
sliced-off caps and place in a casserole just big enough
to hold them. Add broth and the remaining oil to the
casserole.
Cover tomatoes with a plate to weigh them down.
Cover pan and bake at 300° for 15 minutes. Serve cold
or hot.
Serves 6.

WALNUT-ALMOND LOAF

1 cup walnuts, ground
1 cup almonds, ground
½ cup soybean grits (soaked
  in 1 cup vegetable broth)
3 eggs (or 3 tablespoons
  arrowroot powder)

¼ cup wheat germ
½ cup cooked brown rice
¼ cup fresh chopped
  parsley or chervil
salt and pepper to taste

Mix all ingredients together. Mixture should be slightly moist—if necessary, add more liquid.
Bake in oiled loaf pan for 30 minutes at 350°.
Serve hot with tomato sauce or brown gravy (see recipe).
Serves 4.

SAVORY PECAN LOAF

1 small onion, quartered
2 medium potatoes,
  quartered
1½ cups milk (animal or
  soy)
1 cup pecans, chopped
1 cup dry bread crumbs
½ cup celery, chopped
½ cup soy flour

1 teaspoon salt
1 teaspoon sage
¼ teaspoon sweet basil
⅛ teaspoon thyme
1 tablespoon soy sauce
stuffed olives, sliced
¼ cup fresh parsley,
  chopped (or 1 tablespoon
  dried parsley)

Combine the onion, potatoes and milk in blender, and chop with a few on-off motions.
Combine all ingredients in a large mixing bowl and pour into greased and crumbed loaf pan.
Bake at 350° for one hour or until loaf sets.
Let stand 5 to 10 minutes before removing from mold.
Unmold onto serving dish. Garnish with a row of stuffed sliced olives and add parsley at either end.
Serve in slices with brown gravy and cranberry sauce.
Serves 6.

MILLET-NUT LOAF

1½ cups milk (animal or
  soy)
3 eggs, lightly beaten or 3
  tablespoons arrowroot
  powder
1½ cups soft cooked millet
⅓ cup hulled sunflower
  seeds, finely chopped

2 tablespoons minced
  onion or chives
1½ cups cooked lima
  beans (mashed) or green
  peas
2 teaspoons lemon juice
1½ cups hard cheese,
  grated (or diced tofu)

⅓ cup sesame meal
⅓ cup nuts, finely chopped
1½ cup cooked carrots,
  chopped

dash paprika
1½ tablespoons oil
Salt and pepper to taste

Add the milk and lightly beaten eggs (or arrowroot powder) to the millet, and then combine all the ingredients. Pack into a well-greased loaf pan. Bake in 350° oven for 45 minutes. Serve with tomato, cream, or mushroom sauce.
Serves 4.

LOU ANN'S EGGPLANT DINNER

2 large eggplants
2 cups whole kasha
  (buckwheat groats)
1 pound green peas, fresh
  or frozen
vegetable oil
2 large onions, chopped
1 medium green pepper,

chopped
2 cloves garlic, minced
6 large fresh mushrooms,
  sliced
6 large ripe tomatoes, cubed
oregano, salt and pepper
  to taste

Wash eggplants and place in broiler part of oven (cut eggplants in half lengthwise if they are too large for broiler). Broil for 10 to 15 minutes on each side or until well done (you want to achieve a "nutty" flavor).
Cook the kasha (2 cups water per cup of kasha).
Cook the peas.
Sauté the onions in the oil in a large pan. Add the green pepper, garlic and mushrooms and cook until tender. Add the tomatoes, lower the flame and cover for about 10 minutes. When eggplants are done, scoop out the insides and add to the other ingredients except the kasha and peas. Mix well.
Serve with tossed salad, kasha and steamed green peas.
Serves 6-8.

TEMPEH STEAK

½ pound tempeh, cut in thin
   strips, 2 inches wide
½ onion, finely minced

2 tablespoons honey
1 teaspoon sea salt
1½ cups water

Bring mixture of all ingredients to a boil, simmer until water evaporates. Allow to cool. Heat 1–2 tablespoons oil in skillet or wok. Brown tempeh on each side. Drain on paper towel and serve immediately. Other vegetables may be added and fruit substituted for the onion for variation on this basic recipe.
Serves 4.

UN-MEAT BALLS

½ cup ground nuts
¾ cup wholewheat bread
   crumbs
1 tablespoon parsley,
   chopped
1 tablespoon fresh or

1 teaspoon dry sage
1 onion, chopped
3 eggs, beaten (or 3
   tablespoons arrowroot
   powder)

Mix ingredients together. Measure with a tablespoon and form into balls.
Place on oiled skillet and fry; remember to brown on all sides.
Makes 10 un-meat balls.

BASIC VEGETARIAN LOAF
Choose one from each of the following categories:

Protein (2 cups)
cooked kidney beans
cooked lentils
cooked chickpeas
meat analogs (TVP)
tofu
cottage cheese
cooked soybeans

Liquid (1-1½ cups, as needed)
tomato sauce or juice
broth from canned or
   cooked vegetables or canned
   meat analogs
base from vegetable bouillon
milk (animal or soy)
water

Carbohydrate (1 cup)
dried wholewheat
  breadcrumbs
uncooked oatmeal
cooked brown rice
crushed cereal flakes
wheat germ

*Nuts (½ cup) chopped and
raw*
peanuts
cashews
almonds
walnuts
sunflower seeds

Binding
3 tablespoons potato flour
2 tablespoons soy flour
½ cup cooked oatmeal
½ cup cooked cream of wheat
2 teaspoons arrowroot
  powder
2 teaspoons kudzu
3 tablespoons tapioca
1 egg or 2 egg whites

Seasoning (to taste)
sage
sweet basil
cumin
oregano
thyme
rosemary
bouquet garni
parsley
pepper

Salt and/or
Dr. Bronner's seasoning
soy sauce or miso
Savorex
garlic salt
onion salt

*Vegetable oil (2
tablespoons)*
Onion (1 chopped)

Mix ingredients together.
Press into oiled loaf pan. Sprinkle with wheat germ or
grated cheese. Bake for 45 minutes at 350°. Serve with
light gravy if desired.
Serves 4 to 6.

TOFU IN BLACK BEAN SAUCE

2 tablespoons Chinese black
  beans (obtain in Oriental
  grocery)
4 tablespoons wine
6 scallions, chopped
6 cloves garlic, minced

12 thin slices ginger, peeled
2 pounds tofu, cut into
  blocks
3 tablespoons oil
1 teaspoon honey

Combine the black beans with 2 tablespoons wine and
mash lightly.
Set the scallions, garlic and ginger in separate bowls.
Cook the tofu in oil for three minutes.
Add the beans, and cook over high heat for 15 seconds.
Stir in the ginger and garlic and cook for 30 seconds.
Add the wine, honey and finally the scallions.
Toss and cook for one minute.
Serve over brown rice or noodles.
Serves 6.

TOFU CURRY

2 tablespoons oil	2 cloves garlic, minced
2 pounds tofu, diced	2 teaspoons grated ginger
2 large onions, halved and sliced	2 tablespoons curry powder
8 small tomatoes, peeled and chopped	2 cups water
	1 teaspoon salt
1 cup raw nuts, finely chopped	4 teaspoons cornstarch
	2 tablespoons soy sauce

Heat 1 tablespoon of the oil in a large frying pan and
sauté the tofu gently until it turns a golden brown. Add
water if necessary. Remove and set aside.
Add the remaining oil to the pan, sauté the onions for a
minute and add the tomatoes, nuts, garlic, ginger, curry
powder, water and salt. Cook for about 5 minutes,
stirring occasionally.
Mix the cornstarch and soy sauce together, and add to
the other ingredients. Add more water if necessary.
Add the tofu to the curry mixture and stir gently for
another minute or two. Serve with brown rice or noodles. Delicious with side dishes of coconut, chopped
raw onion, applesauce, chutney or raisins.
Serves 4.

TEMPEH IN TOMATO SAUCE

1 large onion, sliced
1 pound tempeh, cubed
1 cup cooked tomatoes
¼ cup red wine

4 teaspoons soy sauce
oregano, thyme, pepper to
taste

Sauté the tempeh with onion until golden brown. Add the tomatoes, wine and soy sauce. Cook for 5 minutes. Season to taste. Serve over brown rice or wholewheat noodles.
Serves 3.

JAPANESE MOYASHI

1 pound tofu, cubed
1 pound fresh mung
  sprouts
3 tablespoons soy sauce
1 tablespoon sherry
½ teaspoon honey

¼ teaspoon Tabasco Sauce
  (optional)
2 tablespoons sesame oil
1 teaspoon cornstarch
2 tablespoons water
pepper to taste

Sauté the tofu, sprouts, soy sauce, sherry, honey and Tabasco in oil for 5 minutes over high flame. Mix cornstarch with water before adding to mixture. Stir well. Serve over noodles or brown rice.
Serves 4.

TOFU VEGETABLE SUPREME

1 large onion, chopped
2 tablespoons oil
½ head broccoli, cut into
  small pieces
4 scallions chopped
1 clove garlic minced
1 pound tofu, cubed
¼ pound mushrooms,
  halved

soy sauce, oregano and
  pepper to taste
½ pound wholewheat
  noodles
½ cup kelp or kombu, cut
  into 1" pieces (optional)
2 tablespoons sesame
  tahini
dash prepared mustard

Sauté the onion until soft, and then add the broccoli, scallions, garlic and tofu. Cook two minutes over high flame or until vegetables are tender. Add water if necessary. Add the mushrooms, soy sauce and seasonings. Cook for one or two more minutes. Serve over the noodles.

Cook the noodles according to directions. Add the seaweed after 4 or 5 minutes of cooking. Drain. Mix in the tahini, and add the dash of mustard.

Watercress, spinach and asparagus can be substituted for broccoli.

Serves two hungry people.

Healthy Desserts _____

NEW ENGLAND RASPBERRY PUDDING

1 cup raspberries, fresh or
  frozen
1½ pounds tofu
2 teaspoons lemon juice

1½ teaspoons vanilla
1 banana, mashed
¼ cup honey or maple
  syrup

Blend all ingredients (in blender or high-speed mixer). Place in a metal or glass container and chill.
Serves 4-6.

STRAWBERRY VEGAN ICE CREAM

3 large ripe bananas, peeled
½ cup strawberries (fresh

or frozen)
¾ cup raw cashews

Chop bananas into blender and blend (no water needed). Add the fruit and blend. Slowly add the cashews

and blend at high speed. Place in individual cups and freeze. Other fruit (peaches, apples, berries, oranges) may be used to make other ice cream flavors.
Serves 4.

PEANUT BARS

½ cup peanut butter
½ cup honey
½ cup lightly roasted peanuts, ground
2 tablespoons soy flour

1 teaspoon dried brewer's yeast
1 cup powdered milk (animal or soy)
½ cup raisins

Mix all ingredients in a large bowl until they reach a pasty consistency. Form into a patty ½ inch deep. Press firmly. Chill and cut into bars.

FRUIT AND NUT LOAF

½ cup pitted dates
1 cup mixed nuts and raisins
½ cup shredded coconut
1 cup apple juice (or other

fruit juice)
2 cups wholewheat flour
1 packet baker's yeast dissolved in water

Chop (or lightly blenderize) the fruits and nuts.
Mix with the other ingredients.
Place mixture in oiled baking dish and let stand for about an hour to rise.
Bake in 350° oven for 45 minutes.
Serve with whipped cream or Freya's topping (see recipe).
Serves 4-6.

CAROB BANANA VEGAN ICE CREAM

4 large ripe bananas, peeled   4 heaping teaspoons carob
⅔ cup raw cashews   powder

Chop bananas into blender and blend (no water needed). Add the cashews a few at a time while blending.
Add the carob powder and blend until mixture is quite
smooth. Pour into small cups and freeze.
As a variation, whole nuts and raisins can be added to
the mix before freezing.
Serves 4.

APRICOT JELL

2 dozen dried apricot halves   1 teaspoon agar-agar
2 cups water

Soak the apricots overnight in water. Bring to a boil.
Pour (while still hot) the apricots and water into blender
(make sure the blender jar is heat-resistant), add the
agar-agar and blend.
Pour into individual containers and leave in a cool place
to set.
Serves 2 generously.

ORANGE FRUIT JELL

1 orange, divided into   or frozen)
   sections   3 cups orange juice
1 pear, sliced   3 teaspoons agar-agar
½ cup strawberries (fresh

Place the fruit in a shallow dish.

Bring the orange juice to a boil and add the agar-agar.
Pour over the fruit.
Place in refrigerator for at least 3 hours to set.
Serves 4.

PINEAPPLE DELIGHT

1 pineapple (fresh or canned
   in its own juice)
4 Delicious apples, grated

½ cup grated nuts
½ cup Freya's topping (see
   recipe)

Cut the pineapple into pieces and place in blender (on
lowest speed so that pineapple is "crushed"). Remove
and mix with the grated apples and nuts.
Place mixture into glasses, filling each about ⅔ full.
Cover with Freya's topping until the glass is full.
Top with a strawberry.
Serves 6.

UNBAKED FRUITCAKE

1 cup seedless raisins
1 cup shredded coconut
1 cup chopped pitted dates
½ cup chopped fresh
   bananas

1 cup chopped raw nuts
grated rind of ½ lemon
enough carob powder to
   absorb moisture

Mix all ingredients together except carob powder, which
you add to absorb moisture. Press the mixture into a
lightly oiled loaf pan and chill. Add whipped cream or
Freya's topping (see recipe) before serving.
Serves 6.

BAKED INDIAN PUDDING

1 cup soy powder
3 cups water
⅓ cornmeal
¼ cup soy granules
⅓ cup unfiltered apple juice
½ teaspoon cinnamon

½ teaspoon powdered
   ginger
¼ cup molasses
¼ cup honey
½ teaspoon salt

Heat oven to 325°. Oil a 3-quart casserole.
Mix the soy powder with the water and heat to boiling.
Mix the cornmeal, soy granules and apple juice together, and slowly add this mixture to the soy powder and water. Cook until slightly thickened, stirring often.
Add the remaining ingredients and mix well.
Pour into prepared casserole and bake for about 2 hours, or until it is a golden brown.
Serves 6.

FREYA'S TOPPING

2 yellow Delicious or
   MacIntosh apples

1 cup raw cashews
1 cup water

Peel and dice the apples, and blend in a blender with ½ cup water.
Slowly add the cashews, adding additional water if needed. Mixture should blend smoothly. Blend for several minutes until you have a smooth cream. Serve over fruit.

Healthy Drinks _____

BANANA PEACH SHAKE

1½ cups milk (animal or   *¼ cup cashew pieces*
* soy)*   *1 peach, sliced*
1 ripe banana, peeled   *several ice cubes*

Blend until ice has been ground and mixture thickens.

STRAWBERRY ORANGE FLIP

2 cups orange juice   *or frozen)*
½ cup strawberries (fresh   *1 cup ice cubes*

Whiz in blender until ice has been ground and mixture
thickens.

NUT MILK SUPREME

1 pint water   *6 pitted dates, 3 figs, or 6*
3 ounces of nuts (raw,   * pitted prunes*
* without skins)*

Grind or chop the nuts and add to the water in blender.
Add the dried fruit.
Blend at high speed for one or two minutes.
Add a dash of cinnamon.
(The best nuts to use are almonds, walnuts or cashews.)

DRIED FRUIT DRINK

4 dried apricots   *2 cups water*
½ cup raisins

Soak apricots and raisins in 2 cups water overnight.
Blend until smooth.

STRAWBERRY SMOOTHIE

4 cups soy milk
1 cup strawberries (fresh or frozen)

1 teaspoon lemon juice
handful cashews
1 teaspoon honey

Liquefy in blender. Chill and serve. Ice cubes may be added during blending. (Other berries may be used.)

SPICY SOY MILK SHAKE

4 cups soy milk
½ teaspoon ground nutmeg
½ teaspoon ground ginger

pinch of salt
cinnamon to taste

Blend in blender. Sprinkle with cinnamon when serving.

HEALTHY SOFT DRINK

Take one cup unsweetened fruit juice (apple, pineapple, grape, cherry, orange) and mix with one cup carbonated mineral water or club soda. Add ice cubes.

PINEAPPLE APPLE DRINK

2 cups unsweetened pineapple juice

2 apples

Blend in blender until smooth. (One banana and 2 strawberries may be substituted for the apple as a variation.)

CAROBANANA SHAKE

2 cups milk (animal or soy)
2 bananas

3 heaping tablespoons carob powder

Mix together in blender until smooth.

APPENDICES

Appendix A
WHAT TO EAT
IF YOU DON'T EAT MEAT
Some High Protein Suggestions

Beans and other legumes—Soybeans, lentils, garbanzos, navy beans, limas, black beans, split peas, bean sprouts, tofu, tempeh. Can be used in soups, salads, loaves, dips, sauces and stir-fried dishes.

Grains and cereals—Wheat and wheat germ, rolled oats, bulgur, buckwheat groats, rice, millet, corn. Especially food for pancakes and waffles, grits, oatmeal, granolas, muesli, wholegrain breads and pastry, and dinner loaves.

Dairy products—Eggs, milk, buttermilk, sour cream, cheese (cottage, cream, cheddar), yogurt, ice cream. Recipes using these foods include omelettes, quiches, soufflés (cheese, spinach, chocolate), soups, breads and pastry, welsh rarebit, macaroni and cheese, cheese or egg salad sandwiches, cheese sauce for vegetables and casseroles, cheese blintzes, pizza, and cheese and eggs added to salads.

Textured vegetable protein—High protein commercially processed soy and wheat products can be used in place of meat in the form of loaves, burgers, steak, chicken, ham, bacon and turkey.

Nuts and seeds—Almonds, pecans, walnuts, filberts, Brazil nuts, cashews, peanuts, sesame, pumpkin and sunflower seeds. Eat them raw or as nut butters; add them to casseroles, loaves, cereals and soup. Nuts and seeds are delicious when eaten raw and unsalted.

Appendix B
FOOD VALUES

(After *Nutritive Value of Foods*, Home and Garden Bulletin No. 72,)
(United States Department of Agriculture, Washington, D.C.)

FOOD	MEASURE	WEIGHT grams	FOOD ENERGY Calories	PROTEIN grams	FAT grams	CALCIUM milli-grams	IRON milli-grams	VITAMIN A Int'l Units	VITAMIN B-1 milli-grams	VITAMIN B-2 milli-grams	VITAMIN B-3 milli-grams	VITAMIN C milli-grams
DAIRY PRODUCTS												
MILK												
Cow's milk (whole fluid)	1 cup	244	160	9	9	288	0.1	350	0.07	0.41	0.2	2
Cow's milk (nonfat, dry)	1 cup	104	375	37	1	1,345	.6	30	.36	1.85	.9	7
Soybean powder (low fat, dry) (for comparison)	1 cup	100	250	52	5.6	244	13.0	70	1.10	.35	2.9	—
CHEESE												
Cheddar cheese	1 oz.	28	115	7	9	213	.3	370	.01	.13	trace	0
Cottage cheese (creamed, curd pressed down)	1 cup	245	260	33	10	230	.7	420	.07	.61	.2	0
Processed cheese, American	1 oz.	28	105	7	9	198	.3	350	.01	.12	trace	0
CREAM												
Half and half	1 cup	242	325	8	28	261	.1	1,160	.07	.39	.1	2
Ice cream (10% fat)	1 cup	133	255	6	14	194	.1	590	.05	.28	.1	1

FOOD	grams	Calories	grams Protein	grams Fat	mg Calcium	mg Iron	IU Vit. A	mg Vit. B-1	mg Vit. B-2	mg Vit. B-3	mg Vit. C
EGGS											
Eggs, large, whole	1 egg	80	6	6	27	1.1	590	.05	.15	trace	0
MEAT, POULTRY, FISH											
MEAT											
Beef, ground, broiled	3 oz.	245	21	17	9	2.7	30	.07	.18	4.6	—
Beefsteak, sirloin, broiled	3 oz.	330	20	27	9	2.5	50	.05	.16	4.0	—
Frankfurter, heated	1 frank	170	7	15	3	.8	—	.08	.11	1.4	—
Porkchops, cooked, with bone	3.5 oz.	260	16	21	8	2.2	0	.63	.18	3.8	—
Veal cutlet, cooked, w/out bone	3 oz.	185	23	9	9	2.7	—	.06	.21	4.6	—
POULTRY											
Chicken, flesh only, broiled	3 oz.	115	20	3	8	1.4	80	.05	.16	7.4	—
FISH											
Haddock, breaded, fried	3 oz.	140	17	5	34	1.0	—	.03	.06	2.7	2
Tuna, canned in oil drained	3 oz.	170	24	7	7	1.6	70	.04	.10	10.1	—
DRY BEANS, PEAS, NUTS											
Almonds, shelled, whole	1 cup	850	26	77	332	6.7	0	.34	1.31	5.0	trace
Beans, Great Northern, cooked, drained	1 cup	210	14	1	90	4.9	0	.25	.13	1.3	0
Beans, lima, cooked, drained	1 cup	260	16	1	55	5.9	0	.25	.11	1.3	0
Beans, navy, cooked, drained	1 cup	225	15	1	95	5.1	0	.27	.13	1.3	0
Cashews, roasted	1 cup	785	24	64	53	5.3	140	.60	.35	2.5	—
Coconut, fresh, shredded	1 cup	450	5	46	17	2.2	0	.07	.03	.7	4
Cowpeas, cooked, drained	1 cup	190	13	1	42	3.2	20	.41	.11	1.1	trace
[2]Lentils, dry, cooked	1 cup	265	20	trace	68	5.3	150	.93	.55	5.0	—
Peanuts, roasted, halves	1 cup	840	37	72	107	3.0	—	.46	.19	24.7	0
Peanut butter	1 tbsp.	95	4	8	9	.3	—	.02	.02	2.4	0

Peas, split, dry, cooked	1 cup	250	290	20	1	28	4.2	100	.37	.22	2.2	—
Pecans, halves	1 cup	108	740	10	77	79	2.6	140	.93	.14	1.0	2
[2]Soybeans, dry, cooked	1 cup	180	208	18	9	117	4.3	48	.34	.14	1.0	0
Walnuts, black, chopped	1 cup	126	790	26	75	trace	7.6	380	.28	.14	.9	—
VEGETABLES												
Asparagus, cooked, drained, pieces	1 cup	145	30	3	trace	30	.9	1,310	.23	.26	2.0	38
Beans, green, cooked, drained	1 cup	125	30	2	trace	63	.8	680	.09	.11	.6	15
Bean sprouts, mung, cooked, drained	1 cup	125	35	4	trace	21	1.1	30	.11	.13	.9	8
Beets, cooked, drained, sliced	1 cup	170	55	2	trace	24	.9	30	.05	.07	.5	10
Beet greens, cooked, drained	1 cup	145	25	3	trace	144	2.8	7,400	.10	.22	.4	22
Broccoli, cooked, drained	1 cup	155	40	5	trace	136	1.2	3,880	.14	.31	1.2	140
Brussels sprouts, cooked	1 cup	155	55	7	2	50	1.7	810	.12	.22	1.2	135
Cabbage, raw (coarsely shredded)	1 cup	70	15	1	1	34	.3	90	.04	.04	.2	33
Carrots, raw (5½ × 1 inch)	1 carrot	50	20	1	trace	18	.4	5,500	.03	.03	.3	4
Cauliflower, cooked, flowerbuds	1 cup	120	25	3	trace	25	.8	70	.11	.10	.7	66
Celery, large stalk (8 × 1½ in.)	1 stalk	40	5	trace	trace	16	.1	100	.01	.01	.1	4
Corn, sweet, ear (5 × 1¾ in.), cooked	1 ear	140	70	3	1	2	.5	310	.09	.08	1.0	7
Cucumbers, raw, pared (7½ × 2 in.)	1 cucumber	207	30	1	trace	35	.6	trace	.07	.09	.4	23
Dandelion greens, cooked	1 cup	180	60	4	1	252	3.2	21,060	.24	.29	—	32
Kale, stems, leaves, cooked	1 cup	110	30	4	1	147	1.3	8,140	—	—	—	68
Lettuce, iceberg (4¾ in. diam.)	1 head	454	60	4	trace	91	2.3	1,500	.29	.27	1.3	29
Mustard greens, cooked	1 cup	140	35	3	1	193	2.5	8,120	.11	.19	.9	68
Onions, raw (2½ in. diam.)	1 onion	110	40	2	trace	30	.6	40	.04	.04	.2	11
Parsley, raw, chopped	1 tbsp	4	trace	trace	trace	8	.2	340	trace	.01	trace	7
Parsnips, cooked	1 cup	155	100	2	1	70	.9	50	.11	.12	.2	16
Peas, green, cooked	1 cup	160	115	9	1	37	2.9	860	.44	.17	3.7	33
Peppers, sweet, raw, medium	1 pod	74	15	1	trace	7	.5	310	.06	.06	.4	94
Potatoes, baked, medium	1 potato	99	90	3	trace	9	.7	trace	.10	.04	1.7	20

FOOD	grams	Calories	grams Protein	grams Fat	mg Calcium	mg Iron	IU Vit. A	mg Vit. B-1	mg Vit. B-2	mg Vit. B-3	mg Vit. C
Radishes, raw, small w/out tops	4 radishes	5	trace	trace	12	.4	trace	.01	.01	.1	10
Spinach, cooked	1 cup	40	5	1	167	4.0	14,580	.13	.25	1.0	50
Squash, winter, baked	1 cup	130	4	1	57	1.6	8,610	.10	.27	1.4	27
Sweet potatoes (5 × 2 in.), baked	1 sweet potato	155	2	1	44	1.0	8,910	.10	.07	.7	24
Tomatoes, raw (3 in. diam.)	1 tomato	40	2	trace	24	.9	1,640	.11	.07	1.3	42
Tomato juice, canned	1 cup	45	2	trace	17	2.2	1,940	.12	.07	1.9	39
Turnips, cooked, diced	1 cup	35	1	trace	54	.6	trace	.06	.08	.5	34
Turnip greens, cooked	1 cup	30	3	trace	252	1.5	8,270	.15	.33	.7	68
FRUITS and FRUIT PRODUCTS											
Apples, raw (3 per lb.)	1 apple	70	trace	trace	8	.4	50	.04	.02	.1	3
Apple juice, bottled or canned	1 cup	120	trace	trace	15	1.5	—	.02	.05	.2	2
Applesauce, canned, unsweetened	1 cup	100	1	trace	10	1.2	100	.05	.02	.1	2
Apricots, dried, uncooked	1 cup	390	8	1	100	8.2	16,350	.02	.23	4.9	19
Apricot nectar, canned	1 cup	140	1	trace	23	.5	2,380	.03	.03	.5	8
Avocados, California, raw (diam. 3⅛ inches)	1 avocado	370	5	37	22	1.3	630	.24	.43	3.5	30
Bananas, raw, medium	1 banana	100	1	trace	10	.8	230	.06	.07	.8	12
Blackberries, raw	1 cup	85	2	1	46	1.3	290	.05	.06	.5	30
Blueberries, raw	1 cup	85	1	1	21	1.4	140	.04	.08	.6	20
Cantaloupe, raw, med. (5 inch diam.)	½ melon	60	1	trace	27	.8	6,540	.08	.06	1.2	63
Dates, pitted, cut	1 cup	490	4	1	105	5.3	90	.16	.17	3.9	0
Figs, dried, large (2 × 1 inch)	1 fig	60	1	trace	26	.6	20	.02	.02	.1	0
Grapefruit, raw, med. pink or red	½ grapefruit	50	1	trace	20	.5	540	.05	.02	.2	44
Grapefruit juice, canned (white unsweetened)	1 cup	100	1	trace	20	1.0	20	.07	.04	.4	84

Food	Measure											
Grapes, raw, American Type	1 cup	153	65	1	1	15	.4	100	.05	.03	.2	3
Lemons, raw (2¼ in. diam.)	1 lemon	110	20	1	trace	19	.1	10	.03	.01	.1	39
Olives, green, picked	4 med.	16	15	trace	2	8	.2	40	—	—	—	—
Oranges, raw (2⅝ in. diam.)	1 orange	180	65	1	trace	54	.5	260	.13	.05	.5	66
Orange juice, fresh	1 cup	248	110	2	1	27	.5	500	.22	.07	1.0	124
Papayas, raw, ½ inch cubes	1 cup	182	70	1	trace	36	.5	3,190	.07	.08	.5	102
Peaches, raw, medium	1 peach	114	35	1	trace	9	.5	1,320	.02	.05	1.0	7
Pears, raw (3 × 2½ in. diam.)	1 pear	182	100	1	1	13	.5	30	.04	.07	.2	7
Pineapple, raw, diced	1 cup	140	75	1	trace	24	.7	100	.12	.04	.3	24
Plums, raw (2 inch diam.)	1 plum	60	25	trace	trace	7	.3	140	.02	.02	.3	3
Raisins, seedless, pressed down	1 cup	165	480	4	trace	102	5.8	30	.18	.13	.8	2
Raspberries, red, raw	1 cup	123	70	1	1	27	1.1	160	.04	.11	1.1	31
Strawberries, raw, capped	1 cup	149	55	1	1	31	1.5	90	.04	.10	1.0	88
Tangerines, raw, medium	1 tangerine	116	40	1	trace	34	.3	360	.05	.02	.1	27
Watermelon, raw, 4 × 8 inch wedge	1 wedge	925	115	2	1	30	2.1	2,510	.13	.13	.7	30
SUGARS, SWEETS												
Honey, strained or extracted	1 tbsp	21	65	trace	0	1	.1	0	trace	.01	.1	trace
Sugar, brown, firm packed	1 cup	220	280	0	0	187	7.5	0	.02	.07	.4	0
Sugar, white, granulated	1 cup	200	770	0	0	0	.2	0	0	0	0	0
GRAIN PRODUCTS												
Barley, pearled, light, uncooked	1 cup	200	700	16	2	32	4.0	0	.24	.10	6.2	0
Bread, white, enriched (1 lb)	1 loaf	454	1,225	39	15	381	11.3	trace	1.13	.95	10.9	trace
Bread, wholewheat, firm (1 lb)	1 loaf	454	1,100	48	14	449	13.6	trace	1.18	.54	12.7	trace
Cornmeal, whole ground, unbolted, dry	1 cup	122	435	11	5	24	2.9	620	.46	.13	2.4	0
Graham crackers (2½ in. sq.)	4 crackers	28	110	2	3	11	.4	0	.01	.06	.4	0
Macaroni, enriched, cooked, firm	1 cup	130	190	6	1	14	1.4	0	.23	.14	1.8	0
Oatmeal, or rolled oats, cooked	1 cup	240	130	5	1	22	1.4	0	.19	.05	.2	0
²Rice, brown, cooked	1 cup	205	238	5	1	24	1.0	0	.18	.04	2.8	0
Rice, white, enriched, cooked	1 cup	205	225	4	trace	21	1.8	0	.23	.02	2.1	0

FOOD	grams	Calories	grams Protein	grams Fat	mg Calcium	mg Iron	IU Vit. A	mg Vit. B-1	mg Vit. B-2	mg Vit. B-3	mg Vit. C
Wholewheat flour	1 cup	120	400	16	2	49	4.0	0	.66	.14	5.2	0
White flour, enriched	1 cup	115	420	12	1	18	3.3	0	.51	.30	4.0	0
²Soybean flour, low fat (for comparison)	1 cup	120	425	52	8	315	10.9	96	1.00	.42	3.1	0
³Wheat germ, raw	1 cup	100	363	27	11	72	9.4	0	2.01	.68	4.2	0
FATS and OILS											
Butter, regular, stick	½ cup	113	810	1	92	23	0	3,750	—	—	—	0
Cooking fats: lard	1 cup	205	1,850	0	205	0	0	0	0	0	0	0
Vegetable fats	1 cup	200	1,770	0	200	0	0	0	0	0	0	0
Margarine, regular, stick	½ cup	113	815	1	92	23	0	3,750	—	—	—	0
Oils, safflower	1 cup	220	1,945	0	220	0	0	0	0	0	0	0
Yeast, brewer's dry	1 tbsp	8	25	3	trace	17	1.4	trace	1.25	.34	3.0	trace

¹Food value taken from: Watt & Merrill, *Composition of Foods* (Washington: U.S.D.A., 1963).
²Food value taken from: Fearn Chart, *Composition of Foods* (Melrose Park, Illinois, Fearn Soya Foods, 1961).

CHOLESTEROL CONTENT IN FOODS,
100 GRAMS EDIBLE PORTION

Food	Cholesterol Content (in milligrams)
Beef	70
Butter	250
Cheese, cream	120
cottage	15
Chicken	60
Egg, whole	550
Fish, fillet	70
Fruits	0
Grains (bread, cereals, etc.)	0
Ice cream	45
Kidney	375
Lamb	70
Lard	95
Liver	300
Margarine, all vegetable fat	0
Milk, fluid, whole	11
fluid, skim	3
Nuts	0
Oil, vegetable	0
Oysters	200
Pork	70
Sweetbreads	250
Vegetables	0

Source: B. K. Watt and A. L. Merrill, *Composition of Foods* (Washington, D.C.: United States Department of Agriculture, 1963), pp. 146, 163.

Appendix C
THE VEGETARIAN BOOKSHELF

Vegetarianism

Altman, Nathaniel. 1977. *Eating for Life*. Wheaton, IL: Quest Books.

Bargen, Richard M.D. 1979. *The Vegetarian's Self-defense Manual*. Wheaton, IL: Quest Books.

Giehl, Dudley. 1979. *Vegetarianism: A Way of Life*. New York: Harper and Row.

Sussman, Vic. 1978. *The Vegetarian Alternative*. Emmaus, PA: Rodale Press.

Animal Rights and Factory Farming

Mason, Jim and Singer Peter. 1980. *Animal Factories*. New York: Crown Publishers.

Singer, Peter. 1978. *Animal Liberation*. New York: Avon Books.

Diet and Nutrition

Adams, Ruth. 1978. *The Complete Home Guide to All the Vitamins*. New York: Larchmont Books.

Airola, Paavo. 1978. *Are You Confused?* Phoenix: Health Plus Publishers.

Bircher-Benner, Max, M.D. 1977. *Children's Diet Book*. New Canaan, CT: Keats Publishing, Inc.

Selected Vegetarian Cookbooks

Acciardo, Marcia. *Light Eating for Survival*. Wethersfield, CT: O'Mango Press. Over 450 healthy raw food recipes. A beautiful book.

Batt, Eva. 1973. *What's Cooking?* Leatherhead, Surrey: The Vegan Society. Over 250 fine vegan recipes. Available from the American Vegan Society, Malaga, NJ 08328.

Bircher, Max, M.D. and Bircher-Benner, M., M.D. 1977. *The Raw Fruits and Vegetables Book*. New Canaan, CT: Keats Publishing, Inc. The classic book about raw foods.

Brown, Edward Espe. 1973. *Tassajara Cooking*. Boulder: Shambhala. Excellent cookbook using simple foods.

Dinshah, Freya. 1974. *The Vegan Kitchen*. Malaga, NJ: The American Vegan Society. A fine vegan recipe book and menu planner.

Ewald, Ellen Buchman. 1975. *Recipes for a Small Planet*. New York: Ballantine Books. Hundreds of high protein recipes.

Farr, Barbara. 1976. *Super Soy!* New Canaan, CT: Keats Publishing, Inc. Good eating with soybeans.

Gephardt, Mattie Louise. 1975. *Meatless Recipes*. Wheaton, IL: Re-Quest Books. For vegetarians who don't like vegetables. Heavy accent on meat analogs.

Hunter, Beatrice Trum. 1974. *Whole-Grain Baking Sampler*. New Canaan, CT: Keats Publishing, Inc. Everything you wanted to know about baking healthy breads, rolls, crackers and cookies.

Hurd, Frank J. and Hurd, Rosalie. 1968. *Ten Talents*. Chisholm, MN: Published by the authors. The classic recipe book for healthy vegetarian eating.

Katzen, Mollie. 1977. *The Moosewood Cookbook*. Berkeley: Ten Speed Press. Lots of delicious recipes from a fine vegetarian restaurant.

Kulvinskas, Viktoras. *Love Your Body*. Wethersfield, CT: O'Mango Press. All about raw food and sprouts.

Lovejoy, Marie. 1978. *International Vegetarian Cuisine*. Wheaton, IL: Quest Books. Over 300 exotic recipes from fifty countries.

Richmond, Sonya. 1965. *International Vegetarian Cookery*. New York: Arco Publishing Co. Good eating with a planetary perspective.

Robertson, Laurel with Carol Flinders and Bronwen Godfrey. 1978. *Laurel's Kitchen*. New York: Bantam Books. Hundreds of delicious recipes plus reliable nutritional guidance. *Highly recommended*.

Shurtleff, William and Aoyagi, Akiko. *The Book of Tofu, The Book of Miso, The Book of Tempeh, The Book of Kudzu*. Brookline MA: Autumn Press. Everything you wanted to know about these exotic and healthy foods.

Medicinal Plants

Hylton, William H. 1974. *The Rodale Herb Book*. Emmaus, PA: The Rodale Press.

Law, Donald. 1973. *The Complete Herbal Encyclopedia*. New York: St. Martin's Press.

Lust, John. 1974. *The Herb Book*. New York: Bantam Books.

Rohde, Eleanor Sinclair. 1969. *A Garden of Herbs*, New York: Dover Publications.

Appendix D
VEGETARIAN CONTACTS

Some Vegetarian Societies and Publications

United States

North American Vegetarian Society, P.O. Box 72, Dolgeville, New York 13329. Publishes *Vegetarian Voice*.

Vegetarian Information Service, Box 5888, Washington, D.C. 20014. Publishes *Washington Report*.

Vegetarian Association of America, P.O. Box 86, Livingston, New Jersey 07039. Publishes *Vegetarian Living*.

American Vegetarians, Box 4333, Washington, D.C. 20012

Vegetarian Activist Collective, 616 Sixth Street, Brooklyn, New York 11215

Vegetarian Action, P.O. Box 508, Radio City Station, New York, New York 10101

The American Vegan Society, Malaga, New Jersey 08328. Publishes *Ahimsa*.

Vegetarian Times (publication), 41 East 42 Street, Suite 921, New York, New York 10017

Animal Rights Network, Box 5234, Westport, Connecticut 06881. Publishes *Agenda*.

Canada

The Canadian Vegetarian Society, 1721 Englinton Avenue West, Toronto, Ontario M6E 2H4. Publishes *The Canadian Vegetarian*.

Animal Liberation Collective/Le Collectif Pour La Libération des Animaux, C.P. 148, South Durham, Québec J0H 2C0

United Kingdom

The Vegetarian Society of the U.K. Limited, Parkdale, Dunham Road, Altrincham, Cheshire WA14 4QG and 53 Marloes Road, Kensington, London W8 6LD. Publishes *Alive!*

The Vegan Society, 47 Highlands Road, Leatherhead, Surrey. Publishes *The Vegan*.

Australia

The Vegetarian Society of Australia, 723 Glenhuntly Road, Scarefield, Victoria 3162

New Zealand

New Zealand Vegetarian Society Inc., P.O Box 454, Auckland 1

India

Indian Vegetarian Congress, 1 Eldams Road, Madras 600018. Publishes *The Indian Vegetarian Congress Quarterly*.

South Africa

The South African Vegetarian Union, P.O. Box 23601, Joubert Park (Johannesburg) 2044

A complete listing of vegetarian societies around the world can be found in the *International Vegetarian Health Food Handbook*, available from either the North American Vegetarian Society or the Vegetarian Society of the U.K. Ltd.

BIBLIOGRAPHY

Chapter 1: VEGETARIAN ROOTS

Besant, Annie. 1919. *Vegetarianism in the Light of Theosophy*. Madras: The Theosophical Publishing House.

Boynton, H.W., ed. 1931. *The Complete Works of Pope*. Boston: Houghton Mifflin Company, p. 139.

Buhler, G., trans. 1969. *The Laws of Manu*. New York: Dover Publications, p. 176.

Canby, H.S. 1939. *Thoreau*. Boston: Houghton Mifflin Company, p. 36.

Carson, Gerald. 1957. *Cornflake Crusade*. New York: Rinehart and Company, p. 19.

Clark, D.L., ed. 1954. *Shelley's Prose*. Albuquerque: University of New Mexico Press, pp. 81-90.

Darwin, Charles. 1890. *The Descent of Man*. New York: D. Appleton and Company, p. 156.

Encyclopedia Americana, vol. 27. 1962. New York: Americana Corporation, p. 720.

Encyclopaedia Brittanica, vol. 22. 1967. Chicago: Encyclopaedia Brittanica, p. 935.

Franklin, Benjamin. *The Autobiography of Benjamin Franklin*. New York: The Modern Library, p. 20.

Freshel, M.R.L. ed. 1933. *Selections from Three Essays by Richard Wagner*. Rochester, NH: Millenium Guild, p. 19.

Gandhi, M. K. 1959. *The Moral Basis of Vegetarianism*. Ahmedabad: Navajivan Publishing House.

Harper's Magazine. March 1970, p. 91.

Hastings, James, ed.; *Encyclopaedia of Religion and Morals*. vol. VI. New York: Charles Scribner's Sons, p. 62.

Journal of the American Dietetic Association. December 1973, p. 546.

Krishnamurti, J. 1971, *The Flight of the Eagle*, New York: Harper and Row, p. 44.

The New York Times. May 15, 1979, p. C-1.

Ovid, *Metamorphosis*. 1958. Bloomington: University of Indiana Press, pp. 367-9.

Schweitzer, Albert. 1965. *Reverence for Life*. New York: Philosophical Library, p. 5.

Seyffert, Oskar, ed. 1966. *Dictionary of Classical Antiquities*. Cleveland: The World Publishing Co., p. 505.

Shakespeare, William. *Henry VI*, Part 2, Act 3, Scene 2, Line 188.

Sinclair, Upton. 1971. *The Jungle*. Boston: Robert Bentley.

Speer, Albert. 1971. *Inside the Third Reich*. New York: Avon Books, pp. 74, 146, 154.

Spence, Gordon W. 1967. *Tolstoy, the Ascetic*. New York: Barnes & Noble, p. 115.

Suzuki, D.T. 1932. *Lankavatara Sutra*. London: George Routledge & Sons, p. 213.

Szekely, Edmond Bordeaux, trans. 1970. *The Essene Gospel of Peace*. San Diego: Academy Books, p. 44.

The Vegetarian Way. 1967. Madras: Indian Vegetarian Congress, pp. 155, 68, 141.

Vegetarianism. (Cheshire: The Vegetarian Society U.K. Ltd.).

Leonardo da Vinci. 1952. *Selections from the Notebooks of Leonardo da Vinci*. London: Oxford University Press, p. 375.

Weintraub, Stanley, ed. 1969. *Shaw: An Autobiography*, vol. 1. New York: Weybright & Talley, p. 92.

Wells, H.G. 1967. *A Modern Utopia*. Lincoln: University of Nebraska Press, p. 286.

World Review of Nutrition and Dietetics. 18, 1973, p. 4.

Chapter 2: WHY VEGETARIANISM?

Agriculture in the Developing Countries Within a World Framework. 1970. Rome: Food and Agriculture Organization of the United Nations, p. 515.

Tourteaux et Proteines 1973. Paris: Charles Robert, S.A., 1974, p. 48.

United Nations. 1973. *Report of the FAO Seminar on the Development of Meat Production, Hygiene, Technology and Marketing*. Rome: Food and Agriculture Organization of the United Nations, p. 39.

United States Department of Agriculture. February 1976. *Feed Situation*. Washington: Economic Research Service, U.S.D.A.

Chapter 3: FROM CIRCULATION TO SEX: A VEGETARIAN DIET IS GOOD FOR YOU

Acta Medica Scandinavia. Supp. 433, 1966, p. 46.

American Association for Cancer Research Abstracts. 1976, p. 68.

American Heart Journal. December 1964, p. 842.

American Journal of Clinical Nutrition. March-April, 1954, pp. 80-1.

————. October, 1972, p. 982.

American Journal of Epidemiology. 100; (5) 394.

American Journal of Public Health. 38; (1948) 1126.

American Meat Institute Center for Continuing Education. 1960. *The Science of Meat and Meat Products*. San Francisco: W.H. Freeman & Co., p. 263.

Ayres, J.C., et al. 1962. *Chemical and Biological Hazards in Food*. Ames: Iowa State University Press, p. 144.

Bargen, Richard, M.D. 1979. *The Vegetarian's Self-Defense Manual*. Wheaton, IL: Quest books.

Calif. West. Med. 24 (1926): 328-30.

Campbell, J.R., and Leslie, J.F. 1969. *The Science of Animals That Serve Mankind*. New York: McGraw-Hill Book Co.

"Cancer Causing Drugs in Our Food"; *Congressional Record*. (Senate); March 20, 1973, pp. 5226-8.

Cancer Research. November 1975, pp. 3238, 3521, 3543.

Carson, Rachel. 1962. *Silent Spring*. Boston: Houghton Mifflin Co., pp. 22-3.

Circulation. 42: 1970, pp. 55A-95A.

Daily News. August 6, 1980, p. 26.

Ahimsa. August 1971, pp. 6-7.

Altschul, Aaron M. 1965. *Proteins: Their Chemistry and Politics*. New York: Basic Books, pp. 264-5.

American Scientist. January-February 1976, pp. 71-2.

Bellerby, J.R. 1970. *Factory Farming*. London: British Association for the Advancement of Science, p. 85.

Boerma, A.H. *Food Requirements and Production Possibilities*. Paris: UNESCO, p. 12.

Brown, H., et al. 1957. *The Next Hundred Years*. New York: Viking Press, p. 71.

Chemistry. October 1973, p. 11.

Environmental Action. March 2, 1974, p. 10.

Foreign Affairs. April 1974, pp. 513-14.

Foreign Policy. Winter 1973-4, p. 4.

The Futurist. April 1974, p. 59.

Jonas, S. and Tobis, D., eds. 1974. *Guatemala*. Berkeley: North American Congress on Latin America, p. 9.

Kuppuswami, S., et al. 1958. *Proteins in Foods*. New Delhi: Indian Council of Medical Research.

Leadbeater, C.W. 1970. *Vegetarianism and Occultism*. Madras: The Theosophical Publishing House, p. 34.

Giehl, Dudley. 1979. *Vegetarianism: A Way of Life*. New York: Harper and Row.

MacKensie, D.S. 1970. *Environmental Quality and the Meat Industry*. Chicago: The American Meat Institute, p. 1.

Newsweek. November 8, 1971, p. 85.

The New York Times. September 25, 1974, p. 8.

Proceedings: Sixteenth National Institute of Animal Agriculture. April 1966. Lafayette, IN: Purdue University, p. 34.

Singer, Peter. 1977. *Animal Liberation*. New York: Avon, p. 103.

Sukhatme, P.V. 1969. *The World's Food Supplies*. Rome: Food and Agriculture Organization of the United Nations, p. 6.

Dietary Goals for the United States. February 1977. Washington: U.S. Government Printing Office.

Dietary Goals for the United States—Supplemental Views. November 1977. Washington: U.S. Government Printing Office, pp. 662-6.

Encyclopedia Americana. 1957. vol. 13, New York: The Americana Corporation, p. 87.

Encyclopaedia Brittanica, op. cit.

Hollander, J.L., ed.; 1966. *Arthritis and Allied Conditions*. Philadelphia: Lea & Febinger, p. 937.

Ganong, W.F. 1971. *Review of Medical Physiology.* 6th ed. Los Altos, CA: Lange Medical Series.

Journal of the American Medical Association. February 7, 1920, p. 381.

———— June 3, 1961, p. 806.

Journal of the National Cancer Institute. June 1973, p. 1437.

———— December 1973, pp. 1771, 1777.

Ladies' Home Journal. October 1971, p. 72.

Lancet; 1 (1967): 1103.

Lappé, Frances Moore. 1971. *Diet for a Small Planet.* New York: Ballantine Books, p. 19.

Levy, Albert. 1967. *The Meat Handbook.* Westport CT: The Avi Publishing Co., p. 68.

Marine, Gene and Van Allen, Judith. 1972. *Food Pollution: The Violation of Our Inner Ecology.* New York: Holt, Rinehart and Winston, p. 19.

Medical Journal of Australia 1 (1959): 627-33.

Moulton, C.R. 1953. *Meat Through the Microscope.* Chicago: University of Chicago Press, p. 510.

The New York Times. April 22, 1971, p. 43.

Paddock, L.S. and Ramsbottom, J.M. 1955. *Meat Packing Plant Operation Manual.* Chicago: The American Meat Institute, p. 35.

Scharffenberg, John, M.D. 1979. *Problems With Meat as Human Food.* Santa Barbara: Woodbridge Press Publishing Co.

Science. July 3, 1964, p. 54.

———— February 1974, p. 416.

Texas Reports on Biology and Medicine, 25 (1967): 553-7.

United States Department of Agriculture. 1956. *Animal Diseases,* p. 469.

Vegetarian Diets. May 1974. Washington: National Research Council, p. 4.

Von Haller, Albert. 1962. *The Vitamin Hunters.* Philadelphia: The Chilton Co., p. 140.

Chapter 4: VEGETARIAN NUTRITION: THE UNSATURATED FACTS

Adams, Ruth. 1976. *The Complete Home Guide to All the Vitamins.* New York: Larchmont Books.

Airola, Paavo. 1979. *Are You Confused?* Phoenix: Health Plus Publishers.

Ballentine, Rudolph, M.D. 1978. *Diet & Nutrition*. Honesdale, PA: Himalayan International Institute.

Bieler, Henry G., M.D. 1965. *Food is Your Best Medicine*. New York: Random House, p. 118.

Fredericks, Carlton and Bailey, Herbert. 1965. *Food Facts and Fallacies*. New York: Julian Press, p. 310.

Guthrie, Helen Andrews. 1967. *Introductory Nutrition*. St. Louis: C. V. Mosby Co., p. 30.

The Journal of Nutrition 3 (July 1955): 403-7.

Leverton, R. and Albanese, A.A., eds. 1959. *Protein and Amino Acid Nutrition*. New York: Academic Press, p. 477.

Manual of Nutrition. 1970. London: Ministry of Agriculture, Fisheries and Food, p. 20.

National Academy of Sciences. 1980. *Recommended Dietary Allowances*.

Orr, M.L. and Watt, B.K. 1968. *Amino Acid Content of Foods*. Washington: U.S.D.A., pp. 54-5.

Pfeiffer, Carl C. 1978. *Zinc and Other Micro-Nutrients*. New Canaan, CT: Keats Publishing, Inc.

Proudfit, F. T. and Robinson, C. H. 1967. *Proudfit-Robinson's Normal and Therapeutic Nutrition*. New York: The Macmillan Co., p. 611.

Review and Herald. February 27, 1969, p. 3.

Robertson, Laurel, Flinders, Carol and Godfrey, Bronwen. 1976. *Laurel's Kitchen*. New York: Bantam Books.

Rodale, J.I., et al. 1960. *Prevention Method for Better Health*. Emmaus, PA: Rodale Books, pp. 334-5.

Scharffenberg, John, M.D. op. cit.

Shute, Wilfrid E., M.D. 1975. *Vitamin E Book*. New Canaan, CT: Keats Publishing.

Shelton, Herbert. 1968. *Health for the Millions*. Chicago: Natural Hygiene Press, p. 13.

Taylor, C.M. and Pye, O.F. 1966. *Foundations of Nutrition*. New York: The Macmillan Co., p. 115.

Wade, Carlson. 1974. *Vitamins and Other Food Supplements*. New Canaan, CT: Keats Publishing.

Winter, Ruth. 1969. *Poisons in Your Food*. New York: Crown Publishers, p. 5.

World Review of Nutrition and Dietetics 14 (1972): 134-53.

Chapter 5: MENU PLANS FOR VEGETARIANS:
LACTO-OVOS AND VEGANS
Chapter 6: SPECIAL MENU NEEDS:
PREGNANT WOMEN AND CHILDREN

Airola, Paavo. *Are You Confused?* op. cit.

Ballentine, Rudolph, M.D. op. cit.

Bircher-Benner, Max, M.D. 1977. *The Children's Diet Book*. New Canaan, CT: Keats Publishing, Inc.

Clark, Linda. 1973. *Know Your Nutrition*. New Canaan, CT: Keats Publishing, Inc.

Meal Plans for Total Vegetarians. Loma Linda, CA: Loma Linda University School of Health.

Register, U.D. and Sonnenberg, L.M. March 1973. "The Vegetarian Diet," *Journal of the American Dietetic Association*.

Robertson, Laurel et al. op. cit.

Typical Lacto-Ovo-Vegetarian Menus. Loma Linda, CA: Loma Linda University School of Health.

Vyhmeister, I.B. et al. February 1977. "Safe Vegetarian Diets for Children," *Pediatric Clinics in North America*.

Chapter 7: KEEPING FIT: DIETS FOR
WEIGHT LOSS, DIETS FOR ATHLETES

Ballentine, Rudolph, M.D. op. cit.

Buxbaum, Robert and Micheli, Lyle J. 1979. *Sports for Life*. Boston: Beacon Press.

Doyle, Roger. 1979. *The Vegetarian Handbook*. New York: Crown Publishing Inc.

Jones, Alan M. 1976. *Quit is a Four Letter Word*. Quantico VA: Marine Corps Association.

Lincoln, Ann. 1979. *Food for Athletes*. Chicago: Contemporary Books.

Morella, Joseph J. and Turchetti, Richard J. 1976. *Nutrition and the Athlete*. New York: Mason/Charter.

Pritikin, Nathan with McGrady, Patrick M., Jr. 1979. *The Pritikin Program for Diet & Exercise*. New York: Grosset & Dunlap.

Robertson, Laurel et al. op. cit.

Runner's World. February 1978, pp. 48-55.

Chapter 8: FOOD ADDITIVES AND THE VEGETARIAN

Chemical Cuisine. Washington: Committee for Science in the Public Interest, 1978.

Food Additives: Who Needs Them? Washington: Manufacturing Chemists Association, 1978.

Hunter, Beatrice Trum. 1980. *Beatrice Trum Hunter's Additives Book*. New Canaan, CT: Keats Publishing, Inc.

Marine, Gene and Judith Van Allen. op. cit.

Chapter 9: MEDICINAL FOODS: HEALING FROM THE GARDEN

Alfonso, Eduardo. 1960. *Curso de medicine natural*. Buenos Aires: Editorial Kier.

————1970. *Manual de curacion naturista*. Barcelona: Editorial Cymys.

Kloss, Jethro. 1969. *Back to Eden*. Coalmont, TN: Longview Publishing House.

Lust, John. 1974. *The Herb Book*. New York: Bantam Books.

Malstrom, Stan. 1977. *Own Your Own Body*. New Canaan, CT: Keats Publishing Inc.

Simmons, Adelma Grenier. 1974. *The Illustrated Herbal Handbook*. New York: Hawthorne Books.

INDEX

(Note: all recipes are listed as one group under the entry "recipe.")

Available for the first time — now yours for the asking!

The complete descriptive catalogue of
the best 220 books in preventive
health care — plus the finest in family
inspirational reading.

**Hardcovers — Larger Workbooks —
Quality and smaller paperbacks**

Direct from the publisher
at prices you can afford,

on subjects such as Avoiding Illness, Living the Healthy
Life — Herbs, Herbals & Their Uses — Special Diets —
Health, Beauty & Exercise — Healthful Cooking, Meals &
Menus — Growing Healthy Children — Books for
Vegetarians

Including outstanding authors —
Linda Clark, Beatrice Trum Hunter, Carlson Wade, Carl C.
Pfeiffer, M.D., Dorothy Hall and Hilda Cherry Hills.

Our family inspirational books feature timeless pastoral
writing in the Shepherd Illustrated Classics series — The
Inspiration Three Library — plus over 90 hardcover and
paperback family classics that you and you family will
cherish for years to come.

Keats Publishing, Inc., Catalog Dept.
36 Grove St., New Canaan, CT 06840

Please rush your catalog to:

Name _____

Address _____

City _____ State _____ Zip _____

We accept Mastercard and Visa